以来，世界经济复苏进度各异，国际局势严峻复杂，我国经济增长保持自有节奏，经济指标持续向好。预计 2018 年，我国依然面临不确定性、不稳定性因素增加的复杂外部环境，国内方面机遇与挑战并存。

(一) 2017 年发展回顾

金融危机以后，我国金融市场复苏稳步推进，金融市场敏感性及脆弱性犹存。2017 年，我国经济增长总体平稳，经济结构不断优化，服务业对经济增长的贡献持续提升，消费需求仍是经济增长的主要拉动力，新动能为经济增长的重要动力，经济增长质量不断提高。2017 年随着全球金融市场货币政策走向转向，资本回流发达经济体的趋势较为明显，对包括我国在内的发展中国家流动性影响突出。尤其是季度末、年末，进入传统财政缴款季节，同时叠加宏观政策调整因素，国内金融市场流动性都会出现一轮收紧态势，这轮态势蔓延股市、债市、大宗商品市场，并出现一定传导效应，使得金融机构利润受到一定影响，实体经济融资成本显著增加。此外，在国际金融危机外溢性效应加强的大背景下，叠加国内经济周期性、结构性因素，内外因素相互影响，形成了当前金融领域内的影子银行、银行不良贷款、企业债、互联网金融、房地产泡沫、地方隐性债务、违法违规集资等“灰犀牛”风险隐患，跨市场、产品关联和机构关联的金融市场特征埋藏系统性金融风险隐患。

(二) 2018 年预测分析

党的十九大报告提出“我国经济已由高速增长阶段转向高质量发展阶段”。2018 年我国发展已经站在一个新的起点，将更强调质量、效率、公平及可持续性，致力于逐步解决发展不平衡不充分的一些突出问题。3 月 5 日，李克强总理在第十三届全国人民代表大会上作政府工作报告，强调坚持稳中求进的总基调，按照高质量的要求发展，坚持以供给侧结构性改革为主线，推动质量变革、效率变革、动力变革。设定 2018 年的发展预期主要目标，国内生产总值增长 6.5%左右；居民消费价格涨幅 3%左右；城镇新增就业 1 100 万人以上；居民收入增长和经济增长基本同步；进出口稳中向好，国际收支基本平衡；单位国内生产总值能耗下降 3%以上，主要污染物排放量继续下降；供给侧结构性改革取得实质性进展，宏观杠杆率保持基本稳定，各类风险有序有效防控等。虽然现行供给侧结构性改革已经取得了一定成效，然而未来的供给侧结构性改革工作难度将不断加大，进入攻坚阶段。

去产能方面，随着落后产能已基本退出，加上上游产品价格回升，企业去产能意愿受到影响；新产能释放方面，企业生产质量和效益还存在改善空间，社会创新创业水平有待进一步提高。去杠杆方面，降低政府负债水平，涉及金融体制改革，防范金融风险难度加大。去库存方面，商业地产及一些三、四线城市和县城住宅去库存压力犹存，房地产市场平稳健康发展长效机制和基础性制度尚未建立，住房租赁市场发展迟缓。降成本方面，实体经济发展面临较多制度性交易成本制约导致活力不足，而涉及社保体制改革、物流体制改革、税费体制改革，短期内实现的难度加大。补短板方面，生态环境保护任重道远，脱贫攻坚、城乡区域发展、群众就业教育、医疗居住养老等民生领域创新不足影响有效供给增加，对民生领域发展存在一定制约。“一带一路”等国际业务风险仍然突出。

四、中国经济的世界影响力

2017 年，中国经济增速回升至 6.9%，继续位居世界前列。据世界银行估测，2017 年世界经济增速为 3%左右，按此增速计算，2017 年中国经济占世界经济的比重提高到了 15.3%左右，对世界经济增长的贡献率为 34%左右。

“持续稳中向好的中国经济有力地推动了世界经济复苏，有力地促进了世界贸易发展，为世界各国人民带来了前所未有的发展机遇。习近平主席在博鳌亚洲论坛开幕式的讲话，明确了我国进一步扩大开放的一系列重大举措，意味着中国将给世界带来更多的开放红利。”

（一）中国经济仍是世界经济增长的主要动力

近年来，中国经济持续保持中高速增长，成为全球经济复苏和可持续发展不可或缺的发动机。2013—2016 年，按照当年汇率计算，中国国内生产总值占世界经济总量的比重由 12.5%提高到 14.8%，提高了 2.3 个百分点。按照2010年不变美元价格计算，4年间中国经济实现了年均7.2%的增长速度，远高于同期美国、欧元区和日本三大发达经济体2.1%、1.2%和1.1%的年均增速，有力推动了世界经济增长，对世界经济增长的平均贡献率超过30%。

作为全球第二大经济体，中国经济的平稳增长也对降低世界经济波动风险起到了举足轻重的作用，成为世界经济的稳定器。2013年至2016年间，中国经济增速波动幅度只有1.1个百分点，明显小于同期美国、欧元区和日本经济的波动幅度。测算结果表明，2013年至2016年，如果不考虑中国经济的影响，世界经济年均增速将放缓0.6个百分点，波动强度将提高5.2%。

(二) 中国市场是世界消费增长的关键力量

中国承载了全球近1/5的人口，人民生活即将实现全面小康，已成为全球增长最快、最具潜力的消费市场。

近几年，中国最终消费对世界消费增长的年均贡献率已经是世界第一。2013—2016年，按照不变美元价格计算，中国最终消费对世界消费增长的年均贡献率为23.4%，同期美国、欧元区和日本的年均贡献率分别为23%、7.9%和2.1%；中国最终消费的年均增速为7.5%，同期美国、欧元区和日本的年均增速分别为2.2%、1%和0.6%，世界消费市场的年均增速为2.4%。

中国已连续多年保持世界第一大出境旅游客源国地位。据有关部门统计，2017年中国公民出境旅游1.3亿人次，比上年增长7%，国际旅游支出达1 152.9亿美元，增长5%。另据统计，2016年中国游客在美国人均花费约1.3万美元，当年旅游支出高达352.2亿美元，平均每天为美国创造约9 700万美元收入。

(三) 中国进口贸易是世界经济再平衡的重要力量

近年来，中国进口需求迅速扩大，为国际贸易繁荣做出越来越大的贡献，有效促进了世界经济再平衡。根据世界银行统计，2011—2016年，中国进口货物和服务总额占全球进口市场的份额由8.4%提高到了9.7%，提高了1.3个百分点，而同期美国、欧元区和日本三大发达经济体的进口份额下降了0.4个百分点。

2017 年,中国进口继续稳健增长,对世界贸易增长的贡献进一步提高。据世界贸易组织统计,2017 年 1～10 月,中国进口(按美元计)增速分别比美国、德国、日本和全球高 10.4、8.1、7.6 和 6.5 个百分点,前三季度中国进口增长对全球进口增长贡献率达 17%,进口占全球份额提高到 10.2%。

中国还是世界重要的大宗商品进口国。2017 年中国进口原油、铁矿砂、大豆等商品量刷新纪录,分别达 4.2 亿吨、10.75 亿吨、9 554 万吨,比上年增长 5%、10.1%、13.9%,进口均价分别上涨 29.6%、28.6%、5%,对稳定大宗商品价格,拉动原材料出口国经济复苏起到了重要作用。

习近平主席在 2018 年 3 月博鳌亚洲论坛上再次宣布,中国将于 2018 年 11 月在上海举办首届中国国际进口博览会。5 月 19 日,对美国进行访问的习近平主席特使、中共中央政治局委员、国务院副总理、中美全面经济对话中方牵头人刘鹤强调,中国有庞大的中等收入群体,将成为世界最大的市场。这个市场具有高度竞争性,如果想在中国市场获得份额,出口国必须要提高自己产品和服务的竞争力,让中国人民愿意买。中国不仅愿意从美国买,也将从全世界买。

(四) 中国改革开放为世界提供了新的重要机遇

中国的发展不仅造福了广大中国公民,也为所有发展中国家和发达国家创造了发展机遇。中国提出的"一带一路"倡议得到了众多国家的积极响应。目前,100 多个国家和国际组织以不同形式参与"一带一路"建设,80 多个国家及国际组织同中国签署了合作协议。

2017 年,中国企业对"一带一路"沿线的 59 个国家进行了非金融类直接投资 143.6 亿美元,在"一带一路"沿线的 61 个国家新签对外承包工程合同额达 1 443.2 亿美元,同比增长 14.5%,完成营业额 855.3 亿美元,同比增长 12.6%。

中国对服务业和高科技产品的巨大需求也为发达国家提供了前所未有的合作机遇。按照美国商务部统计数据,2015 年美货物和服务贸易对华出口支持国内就业 91 万个。中国庞大的人口规模和平稳的经济增长为来自全球的企业提供了发展空间,越来越多的发达国家企业进入中国市场,加强与中国的合作，获得了丰厚的利润。

“中国开放的大门不会关闭，只会越开越大”，习近平主席在博鳌亚洲论坛上的讲话向世界明确表达了中国的立场。作为负责任的大国，中国秉持开放融通、互利共赢的发展理念，倡导构建人类命运共同体，推动世界共同繁荣，将给世界各国带来越来越多的发展机遇。

五、2018年上海国际金融中心建设趋势分析

目前，上海已成为我国中外金融机构最集聚、金融要素市场最齐全、金融服务能力和辐射功能最强大的国际性金融中心城市，成为中外金融人才和金融机构来中国发展的首选之地。根据《上海市“十三五”规划》的要求，到2020年，上海基本建成与我国经济实力以及人民币国际地位相适应的国际金融中心，迈入全球金融中心前列。为如期实现规划目标，预测和分析2018年上海国际金融中心建设趋势具有十分重要的意义。

(一) 提升金融服务效率

党的十九大报告中指出，当前我国社会的主要矛盾是人民日益增长的美好生活需要和不平衡不充分发展之间的矛盾。在产业结构上，表现为服务业，尤其是现代服务业发展相对于制造业的不平衡不充分。从需求结构看，表现为消费相对于投资的不平衡不充分。从增长动能上看，创新的关键作用发挥得不平衡不充分。上海在建设国际金融中心的过程中，金融业应从以往注重传统行业转向为现代服务业和先进制造业服务，从以往主要为生产者服务转向更多地为消费者服务，从以往动员储蓄、推动大规模投资的粗放式金融发展模式转向利用金融科技、高效配置金融资源的集约型金融发展模式，切实提升金融服务效率。

(二) 建设金融稳定体系

金融作为现代经济的核心，在促进经济结构调整、支持经济发展、维护社会稳定等方面，发挥着重要作用。2017年7月，全国金融工作会议宣布设立

国务院金融稳定发展委员会,这是中国进行金融稳定体系建设的重大决定,旨在加强金融监管协调、补齐监管短板,强化人民银行宏观审慎管理和系统性风险防范职责,落实金融监管部门监管职责,并强化监管问责,确保金融安全与稳定发展。上海在建设国际金融中心的过程中,要追赶传统国际金融中心,必须积极推动经济金融体制改革,构建完善、稳定、透明的金融体系和市场规则,必须推动金融法治建设,提供公正、公开、公平的法治环境,必须努力提高城市发展配套能力,提升与国际金融中心发展相匹配的城市服务水平。

(三) 支持实体经济发展

实体经济是金融的根基,金融是实体经济的血脉。党的十九大报告指出,要深化金融体制改革,增强金融服务实体经济能力。强调让金融回归本源,服从服务于经济社会发展,当前和今后一个时期,要把服务实体经济作为金融工作的出发点和落脚点,全面提升金融服务实体经济的质与效。上海在建设国际金融中心的过程中,更需要大力支持实体经济发展,为金融筑牢根基,要把更多的金融资源配置到经济社会发展的重点领域和薄弱环节,更好地满足人民群众和实体经济多样化的金融需求,将服务实体经济的成效作为衡量金融业绩的重要指标。

(四) 完善金融市场体系

近年来,随着我国经济发展和金融市场深化,金融业对外开放取得了一系列实质性进展。开放型经济新体制逐步健全,对外贸易、对外投资、外汇储备稳居世界前列,人民币的国际地位越来越高。2017 年全国金融工作会议指出,要扩大金融对外开放,深化人民币汇率形成机制改革,稳步推进人民币国际化,稳步实现资本项目可兑换。党的十九大报告指出,中国开放的大门不会关闭,只会越开越大。金融市场基础设施是畅通货币政策传导机制、加速社会资金周转、维护金融体系稳定的基础,更是金融中心提升配置金融资源功能的保障。当前,上海国际金融中心建设正处在由扩大规模到注重质量、由集聚资源到提升功能的发展关键期,金融市场基础设施建设就显得尤为关键。上海在建设国际金融中心的过程中，要加快与人民币国际地位相适应的国际金融中心建设进程，有效拓展人民币产品市场的广度和深度，丰富人民币产品和工具，提升人民币产品市场规模和影响力，助力上海建设全球人民币基准价格形成中心、资产管理中心、支付清算中心和风险管理中心。

第四章

迈向开放新时代，高质量建设上海国际金融中心

党的十九大报告指出，到 2020 年全面建成小康社会，实现第一个百年奋斗目标。根据国务院批准的《上海市“十三五”规划》要求，到 2020 年，上海基本建成与我国经济实力以及人民币国际地位相适应的国际金融中心，迈入全球金融中心前列。这一时间点，与第一个百年目标时间点正相吻合。

实践证明，过去 40 年中国经济发展是在开放的条件下进行的，未来中国经济实现高质量发展也必须在更加开放的条件下进行。习近平主席在博鳌亚洲论坛 2018 年年会上发表了题为“开放共创繁荣创新引领未来”的主旨演讲，宣示了中国深化改革开放的坚定意志和决心。迈向开放新时代，上海应抓住历史机遇，先行先试，以一系列创新和务实举措，高质量建设国际金融中心，服务全面对外开放新格局和构建开放型经济新体制。

一、扩大金融业对外开放

习近平主席在博鳌亚洲论坛 2018 年年会上，向世界郑重宣布了扩大包括金融业对外开放在内的若干重大举措。在服务业特别是金融业方面，2017 年底宣布的放宽银行、证券、保险行业外资股比限制的重大措施要确保落地，同时要加大开放力度，加快保险行业开放进程，放宽外资金融机构设立限制，扩大外资金融机构在华业务范围，拓宽中外金融市场合作领域。

（一）“改革开放再出发”，上海加快建设更加开放、更具辐射力和影响力的国际金融中心

4月13日，上海市委常委会召开扩大会议传达学习习近平总书记在博鳌亚洲论坛上的主旨演讲和在庆祝海南建省办经济特区30周年大会上的重要讲话精神，进一步高举改革开放旗帜，坚定“改革开放再出发”的信心和决心，勇当尖兵，做深做透改革开放大文章。同时，市政府召开常务会议部署金融业对外开放先行先试工作，抓紧推进落实一系列金融业对外开放时间表和路线图。上海市委书记李强指出，高质量发展，是从集聚辐射能力来讲，必须坚持功能发展导向，全面增强城市核心功能，加快建设国际经济、金融、贸易、航运、科技创新中心，对外要能配置全球资源，对内要辐射带动区域经济发展。上海土地资源、环境约束日益趋紧，商务成本、生产成本不断上升，要增强吸引力、创造力和竞争力，就必须对标国际最高水准、最好水平，提升制度环境软实力，打造营商环境新高地。上海要按照中央要求，加快建设“五个中心”，加快建设卓越的全球城市和具有世界影响力的社会主义现代化国际大都市，在新时代全面深化改革开放中，更好代表国家参与国际合作竞争，为提升我国在全球经济治理体系中的制度性话语权做出更大贡献。上海市市长应勇强调，从现在起至2020年，是上海国际金融中心建设的冲刺阶段。必须把金融中心建设放在全球经济金融深刻变革的大趋势下，放在国家全面深化改革、扩大开放的大格局中，放到国家对上海发展的战略定位上，登高望远，加快建设更加开放、更具辐射力和影响力的国际金融中心。

(1) 要坚持开放为先，实行更加积极主动的开放战略，加快构建开放型经济新体制。开放是上海最大的优势。要牢牢抓住中央扩大开放的重大机遇，在服务业开放上争取先行先试，提升金融市场配置全球资源的功能；要结合自贸试验区建设，加快建立与国际通行规则相衔接的体制机制，推进高水平贸易和投资自由化便利化，当好服务“一带一路”建设和企业“走出去”的桥头堡。

(2) 要在更大范围、更广领域、更高层次上推进金融的对外开放。充分利用上海自贸试验区这块试验田，稳步推动自由贸易账户体系，跨境投融资汇

兑便利,金融市场化等一系列金融改革事项,确立了适应更加开放环境和有效防范风险的金融创新制度。继续推动自贸试验区与国际金融中心建设的深度联动,在风险可控的前提下,主动服务人民币国际化进程。深化落实"金改40条",加快构建面向国际的金融市场体系,建设人民币全球服务体系,稳妥推进资本项目可兑换试点,不断将金融开放向纵深推进。

(3) 加快建设不断创新、更具活力的国际金融中心,创新、探索金融中心建设的深度。上海正在建设具有全球影响力的科技创新中心,通过科技与金融的紧密结合,进一步释放协同创新的聚变效应。一方面,推动金融融资更加广泛、更加深入地融入创新链和产业链,为科创中心建设提供更加丰富的金融支持和服务手段。这些年投贷联动、科技保险、科技创新板等一系列金融支持政策的落地生根,助推了创新创业种子的开花结果。另一方面,依靠科技进步,加快推进金融创新和产品创新,金融新业态、新模式,成为金融中心越来越大的推动力。

(4) 建设深化合作、更具包容性和普惠性的国际金融中心。合作,拓展了金融中心发展的广度。国家要求上海自贸试验区成为国家"一带一路"建设、推动市场主体走出去的桥头堡,为上海国际金融中心提供了更加广阔的舞台。加快提升上海金融市场的投融资服务功能,主动加强与"一带一路"沿线国家和地区金融机构的深度合作,加强与境外人民币离岸市场的战略合作,打造成为国内外金融资源配置的重要节点。与全球著名的金融城市携手,共同支持"一带一路"项目建设,探索构建互利共赢的金融合作网络,让更多的地区和人民共享国际金融中心建设的成果。

(二) 高质量建设上海国际金融中心,是上海"五个中心"建设的核心

金融是上海城市的核心功能,金融中心建设是上海"五个中心"建设的核心。构筑上海发展的战略优势,打响上海"四个品牌",推动金融高质量发展至关重要。要坚持市场化、国际化、法治化方向,不断把金融中心建设向纵深推进;要坚持金融服务实体经济,进一步推动金融改革开放、创新发展,同时坚决打好防范化解重大风险攻坚战,到2020年把上海基本建成与我国经济实力以及人民币国际地位相适应的国际金融中心,迈入全球金融中心前列。

进入新时代，必须充分把握我国社会主要矛盾变化，必须主动适应我国经济由高速增长阶段转向高质量发展阶段这个基本特征和根本要求，推动金融业高质量发展，为其他领域发展提供高质量金融服务。要服从服务国家战略，紧紧咬住既定目标，加快推进上海国际金融中心建设。要把握市场体系建设这个核心，重点加快人民币产品市场建设；要把握金融机构集聚这个主体，重点集聚总部型、功能性金融机构；要把握金融环境优化这个关键，着力营造“无事不扰、有求必应”的营商环境，继续深化完善人才政策。金融是实体经济的血脉，要把上海金融优势充分体现在巩固提升实体经济能级上，加强金融中心建设与自贸试验区、科创中心建设联动，推动金融更好地服务“一带一路”和长江经济带建设。要在确保金融安全和有效防范风险的前提下，推动金融创新发展。

全面推进上海改革开放的目标任务，不断提升上海金融业的开放度和开放水平，全面深化国际金融中心建设，下一步应重点做好三方面工作。

(1) 不断优化金融发展营商环境，擦亮上海金融服务名片，促进金融业健康发展。主动靠前，做深做细外资金融机构落地配套服务，推进开放项目尽快落地和业务开展。通过持续营造开放、透明、包容的金融营商环境，使上海成为国家扩大对外开放的承载地和重要外资金融机构聚集地。

(2) 深化金融改革，争取更多扩大开放举措的先行先试。2018 年是改革开放 40 周年，在我国新一轮改革开放中，上海将主动担当，加强上海国际金融中心建设和自贸试验区金融开放创新联动，积极争取国家把新的金融产品、业务创新和金融科技等放在上海先行先试，推动金融高质量发展，更好地服务实体经济。同时，做好金融创新风险压力测试，切实守住风险防范的底线。

(3) 以开放促发展，推动国际金融中心建设再上新台阶。加快形成面向国际的金融市场体系，建设全球性人民币产品创新、交易、定价和清算中心。通过开放持续提升上海国际金融中心世界影响力和全球资源配置能力，加快建设与我国经济实力和人民币国际地位相适应的国际金融中心，为促进全球化提供新的机会和动力。

(三) 上海国际金融中心进一步扩大对外开放、先行先试的举措

建设上海国际金融中心是国家战略,上海在我国金融业对外开放方面一直走在全国前列。上海市对照中国人民银行宣布的金融业对外开放措施,形成了进一步扩大对外开放的举措,在六方面争取先行先试。

一是扩大银行业对外开放。如支持外国银行在沪同时设立分行和子行,支持商业银行在沪发起设立不设外资持股比例上限的金融资产投资公司和理财公司,支持外资银行开展代理发行、代理兑付等。

二是扩大证券业对外开放。如支持在沪设立外资控股证券公司、基金公司、期货公司,允许其从事经纪、咨询等业务。

三是扩大保险业对外开放。如放开在沪外资保险经纪公司经营范围,支持外资来沪经营保险代理和公估业务,支持设立外资控股人身险公司等。

四是扩大金融市场开放。如支持境外投资者参与上海证券市场,支持境外创新企业在沪发行中国存托凭证(CDR),争取年内开通沪伦通,进一步扩大熊猫债规模等。

五是拓展 FT 账户功能和使用范围。围绕人民币国际化,建设人民币全球服务体系。争取将 FT 账户复制推广至长三角地区和长江经济带的自贸试验区,以及拓展 FT 账户的投融资功能等。

六是放开银行卡清算机构和非银行支付机构市场准入,放宽外资金融服务公司开展信用评级服务的限制等。

2018 年 4 月 27 日,中国银保监会明确外资保险经纪机构可按放开后的业务范围到所在地保监局申请办理业务许可证变更。上海保监局对英国韦莱集团控股的韦莱保险经纪公司变更经营范围申请进行了审核批准,该公司成为全国首家获准扩展经营范围的外资保险经纪机构。4 月 28 日,法国欧诺银行和光明食品集团等签订投资协议,拟共同设立上海光明欧诺消费金融有限公司,这将是欧美发达国家在中国设立的首家消费金融公司。5 月 2 日,中国银保监会批复同意工银安盛人寿公司发起筹建工银安盛资产管理公司,这是我国扩大保险业对外开放后获批的第一家合资保险资产管理公司。5 月 8 日,野村控股株式会社等向中国证监会提交了设立外商投资证券公司的申请材料,野村控股株式会社拟持股 51%。摩根大通也向证监会提出了在沪设立

外资券商的申请。5 月 9 日，德国安联保险集团总部决定在上海独资设立安联（中国）保险集团公司。

（四）金融业的开放程度要与金融监管能力相匹配

金融中心是一个资金汇聚中心、交易中心，也有可能成为风险中心。国际金融中心搞得好，就是国际金融的重镇。搞得不好，可能就是重灾区。必须始终绷紧防范风险的这根弦，一刻也不能懈怠，始终要把风险的防控放在一个重要的位置上。中共中央政治局常委、国务院副总理韩正指出，上海自贸区应当能够进一步促进上海国际金融中心建设，相关举措还要进一步深化完善。上海金融改革和创新一定是在风险可控的前提下进行的，这是一条基本遵循。

中国人民银行行长易纲于 2018 年 3 月 25 日在中国发展高层论坛上表示，金融业的开放有三条规律要遵循。第一，金融业作为竞争性的服务业，应当遵循准入前国民待遇和负面清单原则；第二，金融业的对外开放，要以汇率形成机制的改革和资本项目进程相互配合，共同推进；第三，金融业的开放要和防范金融风险并重。金融业的开放程度要与金融的监管能力相匹配。

金融扩大对外开放，有必要与金融监管水平提升和金融市场制度完善相适应，与相关金融领域开放相协调。开放金融体系必然会增加金融市场的不稳定性，因此需要完善与开放金融体系相匹配的宏观审慎监管框架，才能有效预防并化解在金融开放过程中可能遭遇的各种风险，特别是跨境资本流动风险。丰富跨境资本流动宏观审慎管理的政策工具箱，包括以降低跨境资本大幅波动为目标的管理工具，如风险准备金；以银行和短期资本流动为重点的宏观审慎管理政策等，逆周期调节外汇市场短期波动，维护金融体系安全和国际收支平衡。

二、探索建设自由贸易港

中国（上海）自由贸易试验区是党中央、国务院在新形势下深化改革和扩大开放的重大举措。2017 年 3 月 30 日，国务院印发了《全面深化中国（上海）

自由贸易试验区改革开放方案》,提出了面向 2020 年的上海自贸试验区改革开放的目标,标志着上海自贸试验区建设进入新的阶段。

(一) 以资本项目可兑换以及金融开放为目标的金融制度创新取得进展

一是以自由贸易账户(FT 账户)为核心的金融开放创新深入推进。自由贸易账户是上海自贸试验区金融开放创新的基础性制度安排,也是最大的亮点。自由贸易账户不仅可以提供经常项下和直接投资项下的跨境本外币结算等服务,还可以开展境外融资、跨境大额存单、利率互换交易等业务。自由贸易账户体系建成运行以来,通过分账核算体系和自由贸易账户,实现了资金跨境流动的“一线审慎监管、二线有限渗透”,为推进人民币资本项目可兑换奠定了重要基础。截至 2017 年 12 月底,上海自贸试验区累计共有 56 家金融机构通过分账核算系统验收,开立 7.02 万个 FT 账户,累计融资总额 1.1 万亿元,账户内资金余额 2 176 亿元。

二是外汇管理体制改革取得成效,人民币跨境使用逐步扩大。在外汇资金池和放宽债权债务管理等方面,通过改进跨国公司外汇资金集中运营管理,完善结售汇管理,简化经常项目外汇收支手续,极大便利了对外贸易和投资。率先建立宏观审慎的本外币一体化的境外融资制度,稳步推进人民币境外借款、跨境双向人民币资金池等创新业务,各项跨境人民币业务快速发展。

三是金融市场和金融服务开放度进一步提高。依托自贸试验区金融制度创新优势,不断扩大金融服务业开放范围,提升金融市场配置境内外资源的功能。一方面,沪港通、上海黄金交易所国际板、上海国际能源交易中心等面向国际的金融交易平台建设稳步推进,定价交易机制不断完善;另一方面,金融服务业对内对外开放积极推进,银监会积极支持中外资银行业金融机构入区经营,证监会、保监会也积极推动证券期货、保险机构在区内集聚发展。

四是金融监管和风险防控能力显著增强。进一步完善金融宏观审慎管理措施及各类金融机构风险防范机制,在推出每一项金融开放创新举措的同时都建立了相应的金融监管制度。例如,中国人民银行上海总部会同相关部门建立了跨部门的跨境资金监测分析与应急协调机制，加强对跨境资金流动的监测和风险防控；上海银监局推动建立涵盖销售、投诉、查处等全流程的银行业消费者权益保护体系；市金融办会同有关部门制定上海市金融综合监管实施细则，加快建立信息互联共享的综合监管模式。

（二）上海自贸试验区金融开放创新仍需不断深化

金融开放创新是自贸试验区开放试验的重中之重，上海自贸试验区尽管已经取得很大进展，但离资本项目可兑换和金融服务业开放的目标还有较大差距。“金改 40 条”仍有部分项目尚未出台细则或推出创新案例，导致相关工作进展迟缓。虽然开展自由贸易账户业务的金融机构已经从上海自贸试验区拓展到了全市，但开设自由贸易账户的企业仍然局限在自贸试验区。自由贸易账户使用主要是在经常项目上，对资本和金融项目交易的限制仍然十分严格，导致一些金融机构对此反馈并不积极。自贸试验区内的跨国公司地区总部对转口贸易和离岸贸易的外汇收付便利化有较大需求，但目前自贸试验区对新型贸易业态的外汇管理政策总体在收紧。

习近平总书记在党的十九大报告中提出：“主动参与和推动经济全球化进程，发展更高层次的开放型经济，不断壮大我国经济实力和综合国力。”“推动形成全面开放新格局。实行高水平的贸易和投资自由化便利化政策，全面实行准入前国民待遇加负面清单管理制度，大幅度放宽市场准入，扩大服务业对外开放，保护外商投资合法权益。赋予自由贸易试验区更大的改革自主权，探索建设自由贸易港。”习近平主席在博鳌亚洲论坛 2018 年年会开幕式上发表主旨演讲时表示，中国人民将继续扩大开放、加强合作，坚定不移奉行互利共赢的开放战略，坚持引进来和走出去并重，推动形成陆海内外联动、东西双向互济的开放格局，实行高水平的贸易和投资自由化便利化政策，探索建设中国特色自由贸易港。

当前，上海自贸试验区建设已进入深入推进的关键时期。中央要求上海自贸试验区继续积极大胆闯、大胆试、自主改，建设成为开放度最高的投资贸易便利、货币兑换自由、监管高效便捷、法制环境规范的自由贸易区。习近平总书记明确指出，自由贸易试验区建设的核心任务是制度创新，要对照国际最高标准、最好水平的自由贸易区，深化完善基本体系，突破瓶颈、疏通堵点、激活全盘，率先形成法治化、国际化、便利化的营商环境，加快形成公平、统一、高效的市场环境。这些要求为上海自贸试验区建设指明了方向。

(三) 加强自贸试验区金融改革与上海国际金融中心建设的联动

上海自贸试验区与上海国际金融中心建设密不可分。上海未来要成为人民币金融资产的交易中心、定价中心、清算结算中心和产品创新中心，应充分发挥上海自贸试验区的制度优势，推进金融市场开放和金融产品创新，以自由贸易账户为载体，加快推进资本项目可兑换和人民币国际化，不断提升国际金融中心集聚辐射能力就要充分发挥自贸试验区的金融制度创新功能，为上海金融中心建设提供有力支撑。

一是不断扩大金融服务业和金融市场的对外开放。提高金融市场双向开放程度，支持中国外汇交易中心、上海证券交易所、上海黄金交易所等在沪金融市场加快面向国际的金融交易平台建设，拓宽境外投资者，特别是长期资金的机构投资者参与境内金融市场的渠道，推动境内企业和个人“走出去”。

二是拓展金融服务功能。加快探索支持离岸贸易、服务贸易发展的制度环境，建立与自贸试验区相适应的本外币账户管理体系，促进跨境贸易、投融资结算便利化；探索建立整合国际国内市场交易功能的大宗商品贸易综合平台，提高大宗商品交易资金交易的便利性，支持在大宗商品领域开展包含人民币计价结算、跨境双向人民币资金池等跨境人民币创新业务。

三是探索建立人民币国际化。完善拓宽人民币跨境投融资渠道的相关制度规则和操作方案，推动人民币跨境支付系统(CIPS)建设，建立完善人民币资金跨境双向流动机制，推进人民币跨境使用；完善人民币国际结算制度，扩大人民币在金融产品结算交易中的比重。

四是进一步拓展自由贸易账户功能。配合人民银行等部门，进一步拓展和完善自由贸易账户功能，抓紧启动自由贸易账户本外币一体化各项业务，鼓励和支持银行、证券、保险类金融机构利用自由贸易账户等开展金融创新业务。探索在自贸试验区开展限额内可兑换试点，实施启动合格境内个人投资者境外投资试点；进一步优化自由贸易账户资金划转程序，简化手续，提高自由贸易账户资金划转的便利性。

五是研究制定金融服务业负面清单。我国金融市场的对外开放受制于境内制度法律、市场规则等。上海自贸试验区应对接国际高标准经贸规则，要加快完善金融业市场准入负面清单制度，推动金融服务业对符合条件的民营资本和外资机构扩大开放，在防范风险的前提下，开展金融业混业经营，推进金融要素市场的建设。

（四）进一步完善与开放型经济相适应的风险防控体系

金融安全是国家安全的重要组成部分，是经济平稳健康发展的重要基础。在推进上海自贸试验区金融深化改革过程中，要特别注重防范金融风险，建立适应试验区发展和上海国际金融中心建设联动的金融监管机制，加强金融风险防范，营造安全稳定的金融发展环境，这对上海国际金融中心建设具有重要的意义。

一是加强试验区金融协调监管，探索功能监管。进一步发挥国家金融管理部门在沪机构和上海市有关部门组成的试验区金融协调机制作用，加强跨部门、跨行业、跨市场的金融业务监管和信息共享，率先探索中央和地方金融监管协调新机制。

二是支持国家金融部门贴近市场监管。鼓励国家金融部门在上海设立第二总部，将部分贴近市场、便利产品创新的监管职能下放至在沪金融监管机构和金融市场，支持国家金融管理部门授权在沪监管机构将试验区内金融改革试点扩大到上海全市。

三是转变金融创新监管方式。精简行政审批项目，简化事前准入事项，支持金融机构自主创新，加强事中事后分析评估。对于现行法律法规未作限制的新产品，鼓励金融机构自主创新，在充分风险自评估的基础上自主决定和开展业务。

四是加强金融风险防范。根据试验区金融开放创新和上海国际金融中心建设的进程，积极完善跨境资金流动的监测分析机制，加强反洗钱、反恐怖融资和反逃税“三反”工作机制。针对金融机构跨行业、跨市场、跨境发展的特点，遵循“金融审慎例外”原则，掌握金融开放的主动权，建立和完善系统性风险预警、防范和化解体系。

五是完善金融基础设施体系。稳步推进金融市场中央对手方、交易信息报告库等制度建设,完善金融产品登记、托管、交易、清算、结算制度。统筹协调支付、清算、结算体系发展,进一步加强发行系统、交易系统、清算系统、托管结算系统、市场成员内部系统和监管机构监测系统之间的数据高效处理和传递,提升相关基础设施技术系统功能,提高市场透明度和运行效率。

六是加强金融信用体系建设。引入高水平信用评级机构,大力推动征信机构多元化发展,积极应用新技术发展新业态征信,鼓励开发符合市场需求的征信产品。加强金融消费者权益保护,建立健全保护金融消费者权益工作机制,探索多元化金融消费纠纷解决模式,建立多部门的对接机制,将消费者保护范围扩展到新兴金融领域。

三、建设全球科创中心城市

建设具有全球影响力的科技创新中心,是上海实施创新驱动发展战略的重要载体。习近平总书记指出,上海要着力加强全面深化改革开放各项措施系统集成,着力加快具有全球影响力的科技创新中心建设步伐。中央将上海定位为有国际影响力的科创中心城市,这需要金融更多地支持科技创新。在科创中心的建设过程中,会提升金融市场、金融机构的业务,促进资本市场发展。

加强上海国际金融中心、上海自贸区与上海建设具有全球影响力的科创中心联动,利用上海国际金融中心的金融资源优势,为上海建设全球科创中心提供资本支持和金融创新服务。在科创中心建设过程中,也会提升上海国际金融中心的机构集聚水平,推进投贷联动、融资担保等金融产品创新,促进科技金融及多层次资本市场的深化发展。

(一) 优化金融服务科创中心建设的生态环境

2017 年,上海市发布了《上海银行业支持上海科创中心建设的行动方案(2017—2020 年)》,明确了银行业支持科创中心建设的发展策略、重点任务和规划目标，明确提出“力争至2020年末，上海辖内科技型企业贷款余额达到2 700亿元左右，较2016年末增长80%，全力支持上海建成具有全球影响力的科技创新中心”。

上海的资本市场也对科技创新给予极大支持。试点“双创债”正式展开，支持非公开发行的创新创业债设置转股条款；出台创业投资基金和天使投资人税收优惠政策；差异化减持政策支持上市公司创业投资基金股东，通过反向挂钩调动创投基金长期投资与价值投资的积极性；研究推出CDR，吸引海外上市的“独角兽”回归等一系列规则和创新产品的推出，营造了对新经济更具包容性的资本市场监管环境，这将为科创企业加速效能转化提供更好的土壤。2017年，上海新增56家上市公司，其中44家属于科技创新企业，占比接近八成。科技创新上市企业通过首发或再融资募得近千亿元资金，为自主创新、产业升级、技术进步提供支持。9家科技创新企业通过发行公司债券融资逾117亿元。15家次科技创新企业利用资本市场开展并购重组，涉及金额468.6亿元。新三板新增上海科技创新企业58家，实现融资38.5亿元。上海股权托管交易中心科技创新板累计挂牌企业达到171家，110家次实现股权融资近11亿元，139家次通过银行信用贷、股权质押贷及科技履约贷实现债权融资近9亿元。截至2017年末，上海已登记私募基金管理人所管理并正在运作的私募股权投资基金、创业投资基金合计在投项目近1.08万个，其中近半数处于种子期和起步期，在投本金超过7 200亿元，为众多科创企业发展打通了“最后一公里”。

（二）以扩大金融开放和金融改革创新支持科创中心建设

一是积极推动投贷联动。2016年4月，银监会等部委印发《关于支持银行业金融机构加大创新力度开展科创企业投贷联动试点的指导意见》，将上海张江国家自主创新示范区列为第一批投贷联动试点地区，辖内3家银行列为第一批投贷联动试点银行。截至2017年末，投贷联动项下贷款存量户数315户，较2016年末增加132户，增长率为72.13%；贷款余额60.90亿元，较2016年末增加34.77亿元，增长率为133.06%。自2016年以来，辖内相关银行业金融机构已累计为391家科创企业提供投贷联动服务，累计发放贷款

139.22 亿元。

二是建立金融支持科技创新的风险补偿机制。上海推动成立"上海市中小微企业政策性融资担保基金",为上海市中小微企业,特别是科技型中小微企业的信贷提供担保,重点支持获得国家创新基金、上海市创新基金、上海市科委认定的创新型企业和小巨人企业。截至 2017 年末,与担保基金合作的银行已达 38 家,年内通过该基金完成担保贷款金额 56.41 亿元,是 2016 年全年的 3.86 倍。制定上海市科技型中小企业和小型微型企业信贷风险补偿办法,对符合条件的科技型中小企业和小型微型企业发放贷款所发生的、超过一定比例的不良贷款净损失,由信贷风险补偿财政专项资金给予相应的风险损失补偿。截至 2017 年末,辖内 36 家商业银行获得信贷风险补偿试点资格,被认定的信贷风险补偿试点贷款产品共 154 种,试点银行累计获得补偿金额 8 598 万元,科技型中小微企业的信贷投入力度得到增强。推动小微"双创"增信基金设立工作,引导金融机构为科技企业提供融资,引导金融资源精准对接科技创新。

三是根据企业成长阶段建立全生命周期的金融支持体系。上海的商业银行借助于金融混业的集团综合经营的优势,提供贷款、投资、保险、基金等全方位服务。如中国银行上海市分行推出的"投贷联动一站通"服务模式,联动中银集团内的各类直投机构,从而实现多渠道多维度的投资服务功能,为企业提供"信贷工厂+投贷联动+跨境撮合"三位一体的服务;建设银行上海市分行的"星罗科创"综合服务方案,为科技型中小企业量身设计一揽子综合金融服务方案,切实改善了科技型中小企业的融资环境。上海银行推出的"科创企业跨越发展融资方案",基于科创企业成长周期前移金融服务,在企业初创期给予信贷支持。专利质押贷款业务,为缺乏抵押品的初创型科技企业解决了融资难的问题,对促进企业科技成果的转化起到了积极作用。

四是通过为科技企业提供保障性服务推动科技企业发展。如上海保险业积极推动科技保险支持政策落地,引导行业配套制定涉及首台(套)保险、科技中小微企业和核心技术人员的专门保险计划。用实财政补贴机制,累计争取科技保险补贴发放约 3 000 万元;用足信息共享机制,通过上海市科技金融信息服务平台共享 2.6 万家科技企业财务征信数据,提升科技保险风险管控水平；推出科技履约贷、微贷通、融资租赁责任保险、生物医药保险、专利保险等享受财政支持的产品系列，形成完善的科技保险保障体系。截至2017年底，科技履约贷累计支持2 242家科技企业共计1 896笔贷款，保障金额达64.94亿元；首台（套）保险保障金额已过百亿元，专利保险已为1 400余件专利提供超过3 500万元的风险保障。

五是与科技园区、风投机构深入合作，依托其较强的经营管理能力和信息优势，共同培育壮大科技型企业。如工商银行上海市分行推出的“科金汇”，以加快科技金融功能区建设为引领，促进区内科技型企业快速发展，推进企业科技成果转化，助推科技型中小微企业经济发展和产业转型升级；交通银行上海分行推出的“科创企业投联贷”，为其下属子公司直投企业、引导基金所投企业、参股基金所投企业因经营周转产生的资金需求提供融资。

六是以金融业扩大开放助力科创中心建设。积极引导外资银行参与支持科技创新。截至2017年末，上海辖内的外资银行科技型企业贷款存量客户数为477户，较年初增加171户，增长55.9%；贷款余额为152亿元，较年初增加60.8亿元，增长66.6%。

四、推进“一带一路”建设

（一）上海国际金融中心是“一带一路”建设的金融桥头堡

上海国际金融中心通过与全球金融网络体系中节点城市的广泛金融联系，发挥其全球化的资本配置能力，满足“一带一路”建设中巨大的潜在资本需求，并通过自身的市场经验及创新动力，积极推动自贸区金融改革创新，努力成为“一带一路”投融资中心和全球人民币金融服务中心。截至2017年末，人民币跨境支付系统（CIPS）吸引了“一带一路”沿线国家和地区的508个间接参与者，覆盖41个国家和地区。通过自由贸易账户累计与“一带一路”沿线国家和地区发生跨境收支2 886亿元。上交所与哈萨克斯坦共同建设阿斯塔纳国际交易所，并与中金所、深交所组成联合体成为巴基斯坦证券交易所的战略投资者。越来越多的“一带一路”沿线国家企业到上海发行熊猫债券。迪拜黄金与商品交易所挂牌以“上海金”计价的期货合约。此外，上海不断加强与“一带一路”沿线国家和地区的金融纽带关系,相关金融机构来沪设立分支机构的意愿明显增强。截至 2018 年一季度末,上海共有来自泰国、马来西亚、阿联酋、科威特等 15 个“一带一路”沿线国家的 5 家法人银行、14 家分行以及 9 家代表处。

《上海服务国家“一带一路”建设发挥桥头堡作用行动方案》提出,“把上海建成‘一带一路’投融资中心和全球人民币金融服务中心”,同时上海也正在成为全球金融要素优化配置的重要枢纽,是金融要素资源优化配置的中心。

1. 融资中心

上海聚集众多的持牌金融机构和央行上海总部、上交所、上期所、中金所、中国银联等一批系统机构和功能性机构,打造出上海的互联网金融中心,为“一带一路”提供项目融资、创业金融等,促进虚拟经济与实体经济的融合发展。上海国际金融中心可以拓展多元化融资供给途径。在充分发挥亚洲基础设施投资银行、金砖国家开发银行、丝路基金提供长期资金作用的同时,大力拓展民间金融、保险和基金行业、国际融资合作、国内银行信贷及债券直接融资市场等多元化融资渠道。

2. 投资中心

上海是中国各类企业主体“走出去”,实现海外投资发展的桥头堡。2013—2017 年,上海实际对外直接投资超过 670 亿美元,规模跃居全国首位,结构明显优化,涌现了一批本土跨国公司。2018 年 1 月,上海共备案对外直接投资项目 78 个,对外直接投资中中方投资额达 10.17 亿美元,同比增长 1 044.1%。吸引专业机构来沪设立功能性总部或区域总部,搭建专业平台和项目对接智慧数据平台,提高“一带一路”建设项目落地效率。推动金融行业的海外机构建设,突破境外金融服务的瓶颈。上海更具备对外直接投资的专业化服务能力,综合咨询、境外投资备案、投资项目推荐、投资地介绍、行业分析、境外投资专业服务等功能,根据投资企业的需求予以双向配对,提供咨询服务。吸引律师事务所、会计师事务所、银行、保险公司、投资促进机构等进驻,为企业“走出去”提供服务支撑。

3. 人民币金融服务中心

“一带一路”建设中应加强与各国的货币流通兑换,强化资金回流途径,

division, financial procuratorial division, financial court of arbitration and financial dispute resolution center in Shanghai, symbolizing the perfection of Shanghai's legal environment. Important progress in construction of credit system: PBC Credit Reference Center has built a concentrated national basic database of enterprise and individual credit information and Shanghai Public Credit Information Service Platform has been launched and put into operation. Big data and other financial technologies are reconstructing a brand-new financial credit assessment system for the market. Constant improvement in payment and clearing infrastructure: RMB Cross-border Interbank Payment System Phase II has been put into operation. The Electronic Commercial Draft System (ECDS) of Shanghai Commercial Paper Exchange, the property co-insurance trading and settlement platform of Shanghai Insurance Exchange and the trust registration system of China Trust Registration Corporation Limited have been steadily launched to the market. Constant perfecting of professional service system: Accounting audit, legal service, asset assessment, credit rating, investment consultation, financial information service, service outsourcing and other professional services associated with finance have developed at a higher speed.

1.1.7 Gradual formation of financial "Shanghai brand" and significant increase in international influence

With the advancement of construction of Shanghai International Financial Center, Shanghai has formed a series of "Shanghai brand" and "Shanghai price" in financial market, financial institution, financial product and service and financial environment and significantly increased its international influence. Examples in the aspect of financial market include "Shanghai gold" of Shanghai Gold Exchange, "Shanghai oil", a type of crude oil futures listed in Shanghai International Energy Trading

Center, SSE Composite Index and "Shanghai-Hong Kong Connect" of Shanghai Stock Exchange, Shanghai Interbank Offered Rate (SHIBOR) and RMB exchange rate index of China Foreign Exchange Trade System (CFETS), Shanghai Key Yield of ChinaBond Pricing Center, Shanghai Marine Insurance Index issued by Shanghai Institute of Marine Insurance and the industrial standard for international settlements released by CCP12, which have formed unique market brands of Shanghai International Financial Center. From Sep. 2018, Shanghai crude oil futures will be taken as the pricing benchmark for the Middle East crude supplied by Shell to Unipec. "Shanghai gold" benchmark price is complementary and beneficial to the existing USD benchmark price in terms of RMB pricing, RMB Kilobar Gold, Chinese delivery, and Asian time zone etc., presenting a gradually apparent influence upon domestic and foreign gold markets. In 2017, the average daily turnover of fixed-price trading of "Shanghai gold" was 4.77 tons, narrowing the gap with that of London gold of about 5.5 tons.

Meanwhile however, compared with London, New York, Hong Kong, Singapore and other top-level international financial centers, Shanghai is still faced with such problems as insufficient innovation energy of market system, relatively low agglomeration of institutional systems, less developed non-bank financial institutions and other market subjects, imperfect service financial institution system and relatively low legalization and internationalization.

1.2 Significant progress of constructing Shanghai International Financial Center

1.2.1 Listed transaction of Chinese crude oil futures in Shanghai International Energy Trading Center

On Mar. 26, 2018, crude oil futures that have been brewing for 17 years were officially listed for transaction in Shanghai International Energy Trading Center of Shanghai Futures Exchange. Liu He, Vice Premier of the State Council, made important instructions for this purpose.

The pricing power of financial products, especially in the international market, is the most important measurement index to determine whether an international financial center has the power of discourse. The launch of crude oil futures marks an important new step toward the construction of Shanghai International Financial Center. The design ideas of Shanghai Crude Oil Futures Contracts can be summarized as " international platform, net price transaction, bonded delivery and RMB-denominated". Shanghai crude oil futures are open to global investors and rely on the international spot crude oil market to attract participation of domestic and foreign traders, thus driving the formation of the benchmark price that reflects the supply-demand relationship of crude oil markets in China and the Asian-Pacific region and the formation of Asian-Pacific crude oil price system.

In 2017, China became the world's largest crude oil importer. Transaction of crude oil futures is an important embodiment of "deepening reform of financial system and strengthening the capacity for serving entity economy of finance" and an important arrangement for the futures market to serve entity economy, and can provide an effective hedging tool for numerous entity enterprises on the crude oil industry chain of China to avoid operation risks caused by price fluctuation.

Transaction of crude oil futures is also an important attempt of "building a modernized economic system and driving the formation of a new pattern of all-around opening-up". The launch of crude oil futures is of great significance for China's capital market to further expand opening-up and can bring important experience for the opening-up of financial market. As the first internationalized futures variety of China, crude oil futures has introduced the participation of overseas investors and explored market operation and supervision experiences for internationalization of futures market.

The launch of crude oil futures marks an important new step toward the construction of Shanghai International Financial Center. According to the plan, Shanghai will be basically built into an international financial center that matches with the economic strength of China and the international standing of RMB; taking the opportunity of the listing of crude oil futures, Shanghai will further expand the width and depth of its financial market, improve its capacity of allocating global financial resources, and continuously strengthen the radiation ability and global influence of Shanghai International Financial Center.

Since the listing of crude oil futures, the market has been operating stably and witnessed a steady growth in turnover and inventory; crude oil futures in prior period have formed a good interaction with WTI and Brent crude oil futures. According to related data, Shanghai crude oil futures accounted for up to 12% in the global oil market in mid-May 2018, ranking the 3rd around the world after Britain (26%) and America (62%), and a situation of tripartite confrontation began to take shape in the international oil market. International energy and finance industries pay high attention to the crude oil futures market of China. The Organization of the Petroleum Exporting Countries (OPEC) points out in its monthly report that the density and sulfur content of 7 deliverable varieties of China's crude oil futures are higher than those of Brent crude oil and WTI crude oil, which means that Shanghai crude oil futures provide a "more useful" oil price benchmark for the region. From Sep. 2018, Shanghai crude oil futures will be taken as the pricing benchmark for the Middle East crude supplied by Shell to Unipec.

1.2.2 Incorporation of China's A-share into MSCI Emerging Markets Index

MSCI, an international share index research and analysis company, decides to incorporate China's A-share into MSCI Emerging Markets Index and MSCI ACWI Index from June 2018, making it a constituent of international advanced share indexes.

MSCI said that the decision to incorporate China's A-share gained wide support from international institutional investors MSCI had consulted. "International investors have 'hugged' the positive progress China's A-share market has made in accessibility over the past few years, and in particular, the interconnection between Mainland China and Hong Kong is a decisive factor." This is mainly because the interconnection mechanism between Mainland China and Hong Kong has developed positively and Chinese exchanges have relaxed their restriction on prior approval of global financial products concerning A-share. There are 234 individual A-shares first to be incorporated into MSCI Emerging Markets Index, and these newly incorporated A-shares will account for 1.26% and 0.39% in MSCI China Index and MSCI Emerging Markets Index respectively.

MSCI's incorporation of China's A-share into MSCI Emerging Markets Index is an important time point. Though the initial weight of A-share is relatively low, this incorporation marks the beginning of Chinese market to expand its weight in international investment portfolio and complies with the scale and significance of China's stock market and economic volume. It is also favorable for the internationalization process of Renminbi to become a global investment currency. At present, the aggregate market value of Shanghai and Hong Kong markets is approximately USD 7.5 trillion, only second to America.

1.2.3 Immigration of CCDC's five major functional platforms into Shanghai

China Central Depository & Clearing Co., Ltd. (CCDC) announced on Dec. 4, 2017 to officially set up the Shanghai headquarter and to immigrate its five major functional platforms, i.e. the cross-border RMB bond issuance center, the cross-border RMB bond settlement center, CCDC Collateral Management Service Center, ChinaBond Pricing Center, and Shanghai Data Service Center, into Shanghai so as to serve the global RMB bond market.

CCDC is the national core financial infrastructure, and central depository system is the footstone for the operation of bond market and the portal for the opening-up of financial market. CCDC's establishing Shanghai headquarter is a great deployment for overall connection to the construction of Shanghai International Financial Center and an important measure for innovative development of China's bond market which helps further enhance the function of Shanghai's financial market as a hub in liquidity management and risk control and strengthen the pricing power, influence and resource allocation ability of Shanghai in the world.

On the same day, the CCDC Collateral Management Service Center was also set up and the Shanghai Key Yield (SKY) curve was released. The release of the SKY curve will draw more attention from global investors of China's financial market and better extend the influence of Shanghai International Financial Center.

1.2.4 Settlement in Shanghai of and release of the first international standard of central counterparty clearing industry by Global Association of Central Counterparties

In Nov. 2017, the Global Association of Central Counterparties (CCP12) released in Shanghai the first international standard of the central counterparty clearing industry (the Template on Public Quantitative Disclosure), forcefully pushing the construction of Shanghai International Financial Center to a new development level.

As the first international financial organization settling in Shanghai, CCP12 was formally put into operation in Jan. 2017. The settlement of CCP12 in Shanghai has filled up the blank of Shanghai International Financial Center in the standard configuration of incorporating an international financial organization, enriched the layers of various financial entities in Shanghai's financial market, raised the energy level of Shanghai International Financial Center and accelerated the aggregation of various international financial resources toward Shanghai.

According to international experiences, it is necessary to converge four categories of indispensable international financial entities to establish the position of an international financial center, i. e. Category I: international financial market institutes, mainly including international commercial banks, investment banks and fund companies, which are main institutes engaged in financial product innovation, investment and financing service and market expansion; Category II: international financial market infrastructure, mainly including institutes that exercise the functions of financial trading, registration and custody, clearing and settlement, payment, information report library, etc., which are important guarantees for the effective and safe operation of economic and financial systems; Category III: international financial industry associations, e. g. International Swaps and Derivatives Association (ISDA), World Federation of Exchanges (WFE), etc., which are the link for communication between different market participating organizations and regulatory agencies and the important strength to promote reform of financial markets and formulation of industrial standards; and Category IV: international regulatory agencies, e. g. Committee on Payments and Market Infrastructures,

Basel Committee on Banking Supervision, etc., which are the top-level design agencies of international financial systems and rules.

The competition among international financial centers has always been embodied in their respective influence on the formulation of international financial rules. For example, International Swaps and Derivatives Association, headquartered in New York and one of the major industry associations of the international OTC derivative market, has formulated the ISDA Master Agreement, an international standard agreement for OTC bilateral transactions which has become an agreement commonly implemented in international financial transactions; International Capital Market Association, an international self-regulatory organization of capital markets participants headquartered in Zurich, has formulated the self-regulation frame rules for market management which have become an important basis for the development of international bond market; World Federation of Exchanges, headquartered in London, is the world's most important industry association for exchanges. It can be seen that it is crucial to be the maker of international financial systems and rules in the competition among international financial markets and international financial centers.

As the first global trade organization of Central Counterparty (CCP) clearing institutes and the key partner of Financial Stability Board, Bank for International Settlements, International Organization of Securities Commissions and other international regulatory agencies, CCP12 is composed of 36 leading central counterparty clearing institutes including London Clearing House, Options Clearing Corporation, Shanghai Clearing House, CME Clearing, Eurex Clearing, etc. CCP12's launch of the first international standard for central counterparty clearing industry in Shanghai indicates that Shanghai International Financial Center has gradually created a soft market environment to coordinate, promote and release international industrial standards and can participate directly and deeply in formulating international industrial standards, which is of great strategic significance for improving the influence and soft competitive strength of Shanghai's financial market in global financial market.

International experiences show that as the link for communication between markets and regulatory agencies, CCP12 is an important strength to establish industrial standards, propose regulatory systems and influence guiding functions of international rules. The years to come are a critical period for in-depth reform of global financial market. With the aid of CCP12, Shanghai International Financial Center is expected to expand its approach and depth of participation in making international financial rules and further improve its international influence. At present, CCP12 has set up three standing committees on risk, policy and operation and a platform for close communication between major international financial markets and regulatory agencies, and meanwhile gradually attracted many senior financial experts from international financial institutions. This can help accelerate aggregation of international high end financial talents and resources toward Shanghai International Financial Center, further improve the competitive strength of Shanghai in the financial system, infrastructure, human capital, city reputation and business environment, and continuously serve the goal of developing Shanghai International Financial Center into one of top global financial centers by 2020.

1.2.5 Establishment of Shanghai Financial Court

After the 2017 National Financial Work Conference, the Supreme People's Court and the Supreme People's Procuratorate further identified the juridical policy for the financial field: the Supreme People's Court issued the *Several Opinions concerning the Further Strengthening of Financial Trial Work* and proposed 30 pieces of opinions to guarantee virtuous cycle and healthy development of economy and finance and promote the formation of a uniform and perfect financial law system; the Supreme People's Procuratorate required improving the ability of financial prosecution, maintaining financial order by law, ensuring financial security of the state to provide forceful judicatory guarantee for financial reform and development.

On Apr. 25,2018, based on the *Scheme of Forming Shanghai Financial Court* adopted at the first meeting of the Central Comprehensively Deepening Reforms Commission, Zhou Qiang, President of the Supreme People's Court made an explanation to the *Decision of the Standing Committee of the National People's Congress on Forming the Shanghai Financial Court* (*Draft*) at the 2nd Meeting of the Standing Committee of the 13th National People's Congress of the People's Republic of China. From that time on, Shanghai Financial Court has the specific jurisdiction over financial commercial cases and finance-associated administrative cases that are originally under the jurisdiction of intermediate people's court, and these cases are to be determined by the Supreme People's Procuratorate.

The establishment of the financial court is another innovation of China's judicial system after the setup of the net court and intellectual property court. Shanghai is the gathering place of numerous banks, insurance companies, securities companies, fund companies and various enterprises engaged in emerging financial derivative service, and especially the place where Shanghai Stock Exchange is located. Huge amounts of financial companies are involved in complex financial disputes, and therefore, public service for financial right relief is badly needed. The establishment of a unified financial court to conduct concentrated jurisdiction of financial cases and promote the reform of financial judicial system and mechanism can help improve the professional level of financial jurisdiction and build a fair, effective and authoritative financial judicial system. Earlier in 2008, Shanghai Pudong New Area established a financial courtroom; in May 2017, financial court pilot program was launched in divisional courts of Shanghai. The establishment of Shanghai Financial Court this time is an inevitable outcome under the reform tendency of Shanghai's court.

A perfect financial ecology must have a transparent system and open supervision. Fair and convenient judicial system is also an important part for financial service. The establishment of Shanghai Financial Court to provide professional judicial remedy for financial issues guarantees fairness and justice and helps China enhance its discourse power and participate in construction of global financial rules. Forming the first financial court of China in Shanghai obviously helps improve the discourse power of China in construction of international financial transaction rules and the international influence of China's financial judicial system. From the horizontal point of view, the financial centers or cities striving to be a financial center around the world always set up a professional financial court to improve their competitiveness. Britain has established the "Financial Services and Markets Tribunal"; U.S. Securities and Exchange Commission (SEC) has set up the "Office of the Administrative Law Judges"; and even Alma-Ata of Kazakhstan has specially established the Alma-Ata Special Financial Court which is independent from other courts.

1.2.6 Issuance of the *Vision and Action Plan of the Shanghai Stock Exchange for Serving the Construction of the "Belt and Road Initiative" (2018 - 2020)*

On Oct. 27, 2017, Shanghai Stock Exchange issued the *Vision and Action Plan of the Shanghai Stock Exchange for Serving the Construction of the "Belt and Road Initiative" (2018 - 2020)* (hereinafter referred to as the Vision and Action Plan). The overall objective of the Vision and Action Plan is to drive and organize cooperation of capital markets along the Belt and Road, broaden the direct financing channel for "Belt and Road Initiative" construction, mobilize domestic and international capital organizations and enterprises to jointly participate in "Belt and Road Initiative" construction, and build a community of "Belt and Road Initiative" capital markets with common interest and destiny.

In recent years, Shanghai Stock Exchange (SSE) has enhanced communication and cooperation in various forms around "Belt and Road Initiative" construction with the exchanges of countries along the line and made positive progress. SSE has organized cooperation forums with such key markets as Russia and Kazakhstan in succession; enhanced cooperation with exchanges along the line; and actively pushed enterprises along the line to issue panda bonds that support "Belt and Road Initiative" construction in Shanghai Stock Exchange. In May 2017, SSE signed a strategic cooperation agreement with Astana International Financial Center to jointly invest in the construction of Astana International Exchange (AIX), and based on its contribution, SSE held 25.1% of AIX's stock shares. SSE also cooperated with Shenzhen Stock Exchange to jointly acquire 25% of the equity of Dhaka Stock Exchange of Bangladesh, formed an union with China Financial Futures Exchange and Shenzhen Stock Exchange, and became the strategic investor of Pakistan Stock Exchange. Key emphases in SSE's future work: SSE will, first, explore and carry out "Belt and Road Initiative" equity financing, further support China Europe International Exchange AG to implement pilot programs of D-share business and broaden the financing channel for domestic high-quality enterprises to participate in "Belt and Road Initiative" construction; second, positively expand cooperation with overseas exchanges in equity investment, etc.; further carry out series activities under the "Belt and Road Initiative" such as Chinese and foreign capital market forums to strengthen Chinese and foreign capital market cooperation; third, further study and perfect the "Belt and Road Initiative" panda bond financing mechanism and support related organizations and high-quality enterprises of China and other countries along the Belt and Road as well as international financial institutions to issue RMB bonds in SSE.

1.2.7 Settlement of ChinaBond Pricing Center and release of benchmark price of bond market in Shanghai

To implement the national strategy of construction of Shanghai International Financial Center, China Central Depository & Clearing Co., Ltd. (CCDC) announced on Jul. 5, 2017 that ChinaBond Pricing Center was officially settled in Shanghai, thus realizing release of the authoritative benchmark price of bond market in Shanghai.

ChinaBond Pricing Center's release of benchmark price of bond market in Shanghai will further consolidate Shanghai's position as the RMB asset pricing center. Bond market is the basic market of a financial market that may help improve the financing efficiency of high-quality enterprises and promote healthy development of entity economy. Settled in Shanghai, ChinaBond Pricing Center can make good use of Shanghai International Financial Center's advantages in completeness of financial elements and aggregation of financial institutions to gain its better development, also can enhance application of the Shanghai Key Yield curve in pricing of deposits and loans and promote development of financial products with ChinaBond index as the object.

1.2.8 Launch of property co-insurance trading and settlement platform of Shanghai Insurance Exchange

On Dec. 14, 2017, the property co-insurance trading and settlement platform of Shanghai Insurance Exchange was officially launched. This platform system provides property co-insurance business with one-stop integrated service including trade matching, data clearing, capital settlement and information inquiry, realizes standardization, centralization and normalization of co-insurance settlement, ensures a safe, effective, fair and reliable settlement channel for market participants, improves the running efficiency and overall liquidity of the market, enhances supervision of transaction on exchange, enables dynamic virtuous cycle of the entire trading market, further advances healthy development of China's multi-level insurance market, and brings first-mover advantage to China's insurance industry in global competition.

This platform has four core functions which directly strike the difficulties facing the property co-insurance business. Co-insurance is a way where an insurance company unites with other insurance companies to jointly underwrite large-scale programs or programs with special risks so as to strengthen its underwriting capacity. The implementation of national major development strategies, the construction of major projects, the breakthrough of major scientific research programs and the "Belt and Road Initiative" construction all require co-insurance to play a more important role. Conventional co-insurance business, however, has been suffering for a long time from lack of business rules, non-standard co-insurance agreement, low efficiency of business information transfer, untimely capital settlement and unsatisfactory dispute resolution, greatly influencing the business safety and efficiency.

1.2.9 Launch and trial operation of the experimental production system of digital paper trading platform of Shanghai Commercial Paper Exchange

On Jan. 25, 2018, the experimental production system of digital paper trading platform was successfully launched and put into trial operation.

Industrial and Commercial Bank of China, Bank of China, Shanghai Pudong Development Bank and Bank of Hangzhou smoothly completed their block chain-based digital ticket issuing, acceptance, discount and transfer discount on the experimental production system of digital paper trading platform. The successful launch and trial operation of the experimental production system symbolizes a breakthrough progress in digital ticket business and is of milestone significance for the development of paper market.

Digital paper trading platform is an important step of applying block chain technology to the infrastructure of financial market. Shanghai Commercial Paper Exchange will keep an eye on and tail after the application of block chain, cloud computation, big data and other frontier technologies in the paper market, drive the paper market to improve its quality and efficiency through scientific and technological progresses, and make more contributions to serving entity economy, preventing financial risk and promoting financial reform.

1.2.10 Shanghai's efforts to become the "Belt and Road Initiative" investment and financing center

Shanghai is actively promoting two-way opening and interconnection of financial market to attract financial institutions to positively participate in "Belt and Road Initiative" construction and enhance the financial "link" relationship with countries and regions along the Belt and Road. With risks controlled, Shanghai will actively drive financial reform and innovation in free trade zone and make efforts to become the "Belt and Road Initiative" investment and financing center and the global RMB financial service center.

By the end of 2017, RMB Cross-border Interbank Payment System (Phase II having been put into trial operation) had attracted 508 indirect participants from 41 countries and regions along the Belt and Road and cross-border payments made by these countries and regions through free trade accounts had reached CNY 288.6 billion yuan; Shanghai Stock Exchange, China Financial Futures Exchange, etc. together with Pakistani partners acquired 40% of the equity of Pakistan Stock Exchange; "Shanghai gold"-denominated futures contract was listed at Dubai Gold and Commodities Exchange. All these are the financial achievements Shanghai has made for "Belt and Road Initiative" construction in its accelerated progress of becoming an international financial center. In 2018, Shanghai will expand the applicable subject of free trade account to enterprises with actual demand in the whole city, including entity enterprises serving the "Belt and Road Initiative" construction and implementing the "Go Global" strategy with international trade settlement and financing demands.

1.2.11 Official trial operation of "Bond Connect" and wider opening-up of China's bond market

In Jul. 2017, Mutual Bond Market Access between Hong Kong SAR and Mainland China (hereinafter referred to as "Bond Connect") was officially launched and put into trial operation. Through mechanism arrangement for interconnection of trade, custody and settlement between infrastructure institutions of Hong Kong and those of Mainland China, "Bond Connect" overseas investors may invest in the interbank bond market of Mainland China via Hong Kong efficiently and conveniently without changing their business habit. By the end of Nov. 2017, totally 65 foreign central banks and similar institutions and 291 foreign commercial institutions had invested in the interbank bond market and 161 foreign institutional investors had entered the interbank bond market through the investment channel of "Bond Connect".

1.2.12 Issuance of the *Guide to the Negative List for the Opening-up of the Financial Service Industry in China (Shanghai) Pilot Free Trade Zone (2017)*

In Jun. 2017, the *Guide to the Negative List for the Opening-up of the Financial Service Industry in China (Shanghai) Pilot Free Trade Zone (2017)* was officially issued. This negative list further summarized the provisions concerning the access of foreign investment in the financial field, improved the transparency and operability of opening-up of financial sector, demonstrated Shanghai's clear-cut attitude of relying on the free trade zone to continuously deepen and widen financial opening-up, and carried out a helpful exploration for further expansion of opening-up of China's financial sector. Meanwhile, the subject scope of free trade account has been expanded to technology enterprises and introduced overseas talents serving the construction of Shanghai Technology Innovation Center, and the functions thereof has also been enriched.

1.2.13 Increasing support of finance to construction of Shanghai Technology Innovation Center

In Sep. 2017, Shanghai Technology Innovation Center Equity Investment Fund Management Co., Ltd. was officially established. As the municipal Fund of Funds guided by the Shanghai government and subject to market-oriented operation, the fund has a target management scale of CNY 30 billion yuan and initial fundraising scale of CNY 6.52 billion yuan. At present, a scientific and technological finance service network covering entire Shanghai has been basically formed and the loan balance of technology-based enterprises in Shanghai has broken through the mark of CNY 200 billion yuan. The "scientific and technical innovation board" of Shanghai Equity Exchange has developed continuously, with the number of listed enterprises reaching 172 and the accumulative financing amount reaching CNY 1.9 billion yuan.

1.2.14 Release of 2017 China (Shanghai) Financial Talent Index

In Dec. 2017, 2017 China (Shanghai) Financial Talent Index was released in Shanghai. The index was officially launched in Jun. 2017 and sponsored by China Economic Information Service of Xinhua News Agency. The index focuses on 7 financial sub-industries, i. e. bank, security, insurance, fund, trust, futures and third-party payment, and through analysis of talent scale, education background and remuneration, it enables all-dimensional dynamic monitoring of the development conditions and scientific prediction of the development trend of financial talents in Shanghai.

Chapter II

Benchmarking of Shanghai and Major Leading International Financial Centers

At present, the status of an international financial center is measured mainly by adopting the Global Financial Center Index (GFCI) system published by Z/Yen, a consultancy firm headquartered in the City of London. The GFCI, which was first published in 2007 and is published every six months, is the most authoritative international financial center index in the world. The latest GFCI is GFCI23 published in March 2018.

2.1 Assessment and Analysis of Global Financial Center Index (GFCI)

GFCI aims to measure the attractiveness of each financial center in the world. In order to achieve this goal, combination of objective indices and subjective assessment is adopted in developing the GFCI. There are a total of 103 objective indices that are called "instrumental factors" derived from the data from authoritative organizations such as the World Bank, the Organization for Economic Co-operation and Development (OECD), and the United Nations. The subjective assessment is conducted by inviting relevant persons from specific financial institutions and government departments to fill in the online questionnaire, and they rate the attractiveness of familiar global financial centers on a 10-point rating scale. GFCI is a dynamically changing index. For the purpose of computation, the above (the latest available) objective indices and subjective assessment are input into a statistical analysis model known as "support vector machine" as input variables to obtain the GFCI values of current period. Table 2 - 1 lists the partial ranking of GFCI financial centers given in the last 6 periods (from GFCI - 18 in September 2015 to GFCI - 23 in March 2018).

Table 2 - 1 Financial Centers in the Front Rank in the Last 6 GFCI Reports

Ranking/ Report	GFCI - 23	GFCI - 22	GFCI - 21	GFCI - 20	GFCI - 19	GFCI - 18
1	London	London	London	London	London	London
2	New York	New York	New York	New York	New York	New York
3	Hong Kong	Hong Kong	Singapore	Singapore	Singapore	Hong Kong
4	Singapore	Singapore	Hong Kong	Hong Kong	Hong Kong	Singapore
5	Tokyo	Tokyo	Tokyo	Tokyo	Tokyo	Tokyo
6	Shanghai	Shanghai	San Francisco	San Francisco	Zurich	Seoul
7	Toronto	Toronto	Chicago	Boston	Washington	Zurich
8	San Francisco	Sydney	Sydney	Chicago	San Francisco	Toronto
9	Sydney	Zurich	Boston	Zurich	Boston	San Francisco
10	Boston	Beijing	Toronto	Washington	Toronto	Washington
11	Beijing	Frankfurt	Zurich	Sydney	Chicago	Chicago
12	Melbourne	Montreal	Washington	Luxembourg	Seoul	Boston
13	Montreal	Melbourne	Shanghai	Toronto	Dubai	Geneva
14	Chicago	Luxembourg	Montreal	Seoul	Luxembourg	Frankfurt
15	Vancouver	Geneva	Osaka	Montreal	Geneva	Sydney
16	Zurich	San Francisco	Beijing	Shanghai	Shanghai	Dubai
17	Los Angeles	Vancouver	Vancouver	Osaka	Sydney	Montreal
18	Shenzhen	Dubai	Luxembourg	Dubai	Frankfurt	Vancouver
19	Dubai	Boston	Los Angeles	Frankfurt	Shenzhen	Luxembourg
20	Frankfurt	Shenzhen	Geneva	Vancouver	Osaka	Osaka
21	Luxembourg	Osaka	Melbourne	Taipei	Montreal	Shanghai

Data source: data of previous GFCI reports

From Table 2 - 1, it can be seen that the rankings of top five financial centers in the world basically remain unchanged, with London in the 1st place, New York in the 2nd place, Hong Kong in the 3rd place, Singapore in the 4th place and Tokyo in the 5th place. Only the rankings of Hong Kong and Singapore are transposed sometimes. It also shows that these five cities are well-deserved world's leading international financial centers.

There are great changes in the rankings of financial center cities ranked from 6th to 21st, which indicating that the competition among the second tier of financial center cities is fairly fierce. For example, Seoul of South Korea once ranked 6th in the GFCI - 18, higher than Zurich, Toronto and Frankfurt and many other famous financial centers in the ranking. But in the next two rankings, Seoul quickly dropped to 12th and 14th places, and then was not listed in top 21 after March 2017. It was ranked 27th in the most recent assessment in March 2018. Shanghai, in contrast to Seoul, ranked only 21st in the GFCI - 18, has maintained a rapid ascent in the ranking since then, ranking 6th in the latest two rankings. It remains in the front rank of the second tier. The ranking of some cities, typically San Francisco, fluctuate wildly. It ranked 9th in the GFCI - 18, and rose to the 6th place in the GFCI - 20 and kept this place for one year. But in the GFCI - 22 in September 2017, San Francisco fell to 16th place, and only half a year later, it increased to 8th place. Cities such as Boston and Frankfurt had also experienced rapid rises and falls in their rankings in a short term.

The GFCI reports, which list the rankings of nearly 100 financial centers around the world, also give each city a rating. As mentioned above, the rating is the result of statistical calculation of 103 objective assessment factors and thousands of subjective assessment questionnaires by use of the support vector machine. The main factors that influence the rating of a city in the GFCI are:

(1) Value of each instrumental factor. The 103 instrumental factors are included into five categories, namely business environment, human capital, infrastructure, financial development and reputation, and each category contains 10 to 20 specific indices. The rise or improvement of these indices values of a financial center would obviously improve its rating in the assessment.

(2) Subjective assessment. GFCI online questionnaire survey forms another category of assessment basis paralleling the instrumental factors, so the scores given by the respondents to a financial center in the online questionnaire survey will have an important impact on the final rating of the center in the assessment. For example, in the GFCI22 assessment, 2,058 respondents gave 23,812 valid assessments.

Since the specific methods and parameters used in the GFCI reports are not made known to the public, it is very difficult to study the changes in the city rankings in the GFCI reports. First, the raw data used in the GFCI assessment is not available. The 103 instrumental factors used in the assessment are derived from more than ten international institutions such as the World Bank, with a total data volume of up to 10 million, and some data sources are not publicly available. If the raw data cannot be gained from the GFCI publisher, it requires a huge amount of work to search data from relevant data sources again and therefore such search is not feasible. Second, the subjective assessment part of the GFCI assessment, that is the score data given to financial centers worldwide in the online questionnaire system by relevant invited persons from financial circles, can only be obtained by the GFCI publisher. Third, even if the data of above two parts is obtained, quantitative analysis of the impact of these data on the change of a city' rating (and ranking) is impossible as the specific model structure and parameters setting of statistical analysis model "support vector machine" is unknown. (Certainly, if there is sufficient data, the parameter structure of "support vector machine" can be stimulated and speculated approximately by adopting the econometric method according to the principle of reverse engineering.)

According to the publicly available data, we can make the following preliminary inferences about the rating mechanism in the GFCI assessment after data analysis and collation.

First, there is an upper limit on the rating which is roughly equivalent to about 800 of London. Therefore, no matter how the world economy and international financial market change, London, ranked 1st, had the ratings close to 800 in all previous assessments.

Second, in the same report, the relative rating of a city in the assessment determines its ranking. It is worth noting that the absolute gap between the assessment ratings of two cities does not necessarily reflect the actual development gap between the two financial centers. Take San Francisco and Toronto for example, their ratings are 724 and 719 respectively in the GFCI - 21, 693 and 710 respectively in the GFCI - 22, and 726 and 728 respectively in the latest GFCI - 23. Since these three assessments were conducted only one year apart (March 2017 to March 2018), it is hard to imagine such a dramatic change in the development gap between the two financial centers.

Thirdly, there is no comparability between the ratings obtained from two assessments. If we study the ratings and rankings of the same city in all previous assessments, it can be found that there are many unconformities between rating changes and ranking changes. Shanghai, for example, got 715 in the GFCI - 21, ranking 13th, while it got 711 in the GFCI - 22, rising to 6th place. Toronto got 707 in the GFCI - 19, ranking 10th, while it got 710 in the GFCI - 20, falling to 13th place. This indicates that the change in ranking of a city in an assessment is more dependent on the rating changes of all other financial centers in the assessment, rather than just its own rating.

Fourth, the ratings have a high correlation with some basic variables. In appendix 4 to the GFCI - 21 report, 25 instrumental factor indices with the highest correlation with the ratings were published (see table 2 - 2), the GFCI - 22 began to publish the 30 most relevant instrumental factor indices. Of course, the final rating will depend on the subjective rating, but the subjective rating data is not made known to public and then is not considered temporarily. Therefore, as far as the existing data is concerned, it can be concluded that the 30 most relevant instrumental factor indices in the GFCI - 22 determine the ratings of each financial center and thus determine their rankings.

Table 2 - 2 Instrumental Factors

NO.	Category	Instrumental Factors	R-squared
1	RF	Price Levels	0.397
2	RF	IESE cities in motion index	0.332
3	IF	Office Occupancy Cost	0.323
4	BE	Government Effectiveness	0.257
5	RF	Global Competitiveness Index	0.256
6	RF	Sustainable Cities Index	0.248
7	BE	Wage Comparison Index	0.243
8	BE	Business Environment Rankings	0.243
9	IF	Logistics Performance Index	0.243
10	RF	Global Cities Index	0.238
11	BE	Economic Freedom of the World	0.231
12	HC	Citizens Domestic Purchasing Power	0.222
13	BE	Operational Risk Rating	0.22
14	BE	Regulatory Quality	0.218
15	RF	World Competitiveness Scoreboard	0.215
16	RF	Global Enabling Trade Report	0.214
17	IF	Networked Readiness Index	0.21
18	BE	Corruption Perception Index	0.208
19	IF	Networked Society Index	0.208

(续表)

NO.	Category	Instrumental Factors	R-squared
20	BE	Control of Corruption	0.204
21	HC	Top Tourism Destinations	0.194
22	BE	Rule of Law	0.193
23	HC	Quality of Living City Rankings	0.189
24	IF	Quality of Roads	0.183
25	BE	Ease of Doing Business Index	0.183
26	RF	Global Innovation Index	0.183
27	BE	Regulatory Enforcement	0.18
28	BE	Global Cybersecurity Index	0.179
29	IF	Quality of Domestic Transport Network	0.178
30	HC	Cost of Living City Rankings	0.174

Date source: Data of previous GFCI－22 report.

Note: In the category, BE means business environment, FS means financial sector development, IF means infrastructure factor, HC means human capital, RF means reputation and other factors.

2.2 Benchmarking of Shanghai and Major Leading International Financial Centers

The world's "major international financial centers" are obviously the five financial centers that steadily ranked the top five places in all previous GFCI assessments, i.e. London, New York, Hong Kong, Singapore and Tokyo. The criteria applied shall be instrumental factors having high correlation with the final rating in the GFCI－22 assessment. Meanwhile, the availability of data is considered to analyze the relative advantages and disadvantages between Shanghai and other international financial centers item by item.

First, a general analysis is conducted. Figure 2－1 shows the ratings of Shanghai and the five major international financial centers in the last six GFCI assessments, with ratings listed in Table 2－3. Although as mentioned

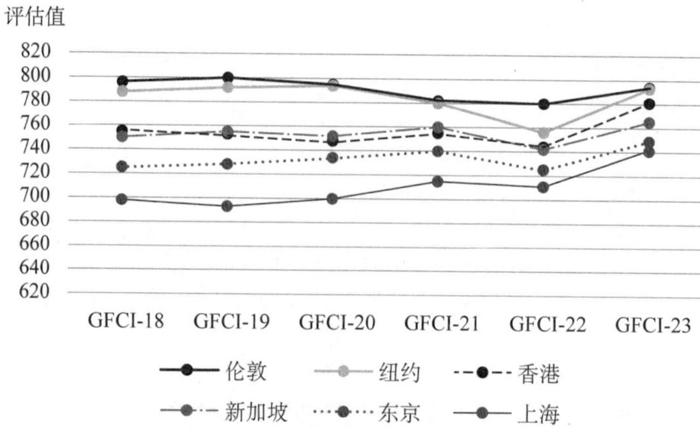

Fig. 2 - 1 Ratings of Part Financial Centers in Last 6 GFCI Assessments

Data source: data of previous GFCI reports

Table 2 - 3 Ratings from Last 6 GFCI Assessments

Ranking	GFCI - 23	GFCI - 22	GFCI - 21	GFCI - 20	GFCI - 19	GFCI - 18	Average
London	794	780	782	795	800	796	791.2
New York	793	756	780	794	792	788	783.8
Hong Kong	781	744	755	748	753	755	756.0
Singapore	765	742	760	752	755	750	754.0
Tokyo	749	725	740	734	728	725	733.5
Shanghai	741	711	715	700	693	698	709.7

Data source: data of previous GFCI reports.

above, the ratings from all assessments are incomparable, it is significant to compare their sums or averages to some extent as they largely reflects the overall situation of the financial development level of each center.

It can be seen from the data in the table that, in recent years the development level of Shanghai International Financial Center is improved rapidly and the gap between it and Tokyo (in 5th place) is narrowing, but there is still a large gap between it and Singapore or Hong Kong (in 4th place). Several highly relevant available indices are selected to conduct the benchmarking according to the five key categories: business environment, reputation and other factors, infrastructure factor, human capital and financial sector development .

2.2.1 Business environment

The efficient operation of modern market economy is inseparable from incorruptible political environment, high economic freedom and convenient business environment. Shanghai is in the front rank in China in terms of these aspects. However, as country-specific data released by relevant international organizations and research institutions is used in the GFCI assessments, China's data is used for assessment of Shanghai. As shown in table 2 - 4, there exists a big gap between China and countries (regions) where the other five international financial centers are located in terms of basic business environment. It may to some extent highlight the real gap between Shanghai and the other five international financial centers including New York.

Table 2 - 4 Comparison of Basic Business Environment

Country/ Region	Corruption perceptions index		Economic freedom		Business environment	
	Score in 2015	Ranking	Score in 2015	Ranking	Score from 2014 - 2018	Ranking
Mainland China	37	84	6.4	113	6.39	50
UK	81	10	8.05	6	7.44	22
Hong Kong, China	75	18	8.97	1	8.39	3
Japan	75	20	7.47	40	7.33	27
Singapore	85	8	8.81	2	8.65	1
USA	76	17	7.94	12	8.25	7

Data source: Website of Transparency International, website of Fraser Institute and website of EIU.

Note: A total of 168 countries or regions were involved in the corruption perceptions index ranking on a 100-point rating scale. A total of 159 countries or regions were involved in the economic freedom ranking on a 10-point rating scale. A total of 82 countries or regions were involved in the business environment ranking on a 10-point rating.

Specifically, China scored 37 in corruption perceptions index (anti-corruption index) in 2015, ranking 84th out of 168 participating countries or regions around the world, at a lower-middle level. In terms of economic freedom, China ranked lower, taking 113th place in 159 countries or regions, indicating that China still intervenes in the market greatly. China ranked 50th out of 82 countries or regions in terms of business environment, also at a lower-middle level.

Table 2 - 5 shows the government efficiency of China and the other five countries or regions. Singapore government has long been the most efficient government in the world, achieving the perfect score of 100 more than once. Hong Kong SAR's government is also efficient. As large economies, Japan, the USA and the UK have less efficient governments than city-state Singapore and Hong Kong, but they still get high scores of around 95. Since 2010, the score of China' government efficiency has increased from 57.89 to 67.79, an increase of 17.1%. However, compared with the highest international level, there is still much room for improvement.

Table 2 - 5 Comparison of Government Efficiency

	2010	2011	2012	2013	2014	2015	2016
Mainland China	57.89	58.29	57.82	55.45	64.90	68.27	67.79
UK	91.87	91.94	92.42	90.52	92.79	94.23	92.79
Hong Kong, China	93.78	93.84	97.16	95.26	98.08	99.04	98.08
Japan	90.43	89.57	88.63	93.84	96.15	95.19	95.67
Singapore	100.00	99.53	99.53	99.53	100.00	100.00	100.00
USA	91.39	91.00	90.52	91.00	89.90	89.90	91.35

Date source: Website of the World Bank.
Note: The perfect score is 100.

Table 2 - 6 shows the control quality of China and the other five countries or regions. In terms of quality control, Singapore has also long been ranking 1st in the world, achieving the perfect score of 100 more than once. The control quality of Hong Kong SAR is also close to the perfect score. As a large economy, the UK has lower control quality than city-state Singapore and Hong Kong, but it still gets high score of around 95. The control quality in the USA and Japan is lower than that of the UK, scoring around 90. China's control quality has remained largely unchanged since 2010, at a level of 44~45 which is only half of that of the USA. This indicates that there is still a considerable gap on the control quality between China and the other five countries or regions.

Table 2 - 6 Comparison of Control Quality

	2010	2011	2012	2013	2014	2015	2016
Mainland China	44.50	44.55	44.08	44.08	43.75	44.23	44.23
UK	97.61	95.26	94.79	96.21	97.12	98.56	95.19
Hong Kong, China	100.00	96.21	99.53	99.53	99.52	99.52	99.52
Japan	81.82	81.99	84.36	82.94	84.13	85.10	90.38
Singapore	98.09	96.68	100.00	100.00	100.00	100.00	100.00
USA	91.87	91.94	87.68	86.73	88.94	85.58	91.83

Date source: Website of the World Bank.
Note: The perfect score is 100.

Table 2 - 7 gives a set of data with specific urban indices in business environment factors: wage level. The data source does not include Singapore. The level of Zurich was taken as 100 in and before 2003 and the level of New York was taken as 100 in and after 2006. As we can see, the wage level of Shanghai was lower than those of the other five international financial centers, only 8.5% of that of New York in 2000. But the wage level of Shanghai grew faster, reaching 18% of that of New York in 2015 which represents an increase of 125% in relative terms. It is noted that during this period the relative wage levels of London and Hong Kong were not improved greatly and Tokyo even experienced a significant decline in relevant wage level whereas the increase in relative wage level of Shanghai was obviously greater than those of the other five international financial centers. This is a disadvantageous factor for the building of Shanghai International Financial Center.

Table 2 - 7 Comparison of Wage Level

	2000	2003	2006	2009	2012	2015
Shanghai	8.5	12.8	11.5	15.1	20.9	18.1
London	64.1	65.6	89.2	69	79.5	75.5
Hong Kong	46	31.1	27.4	33.7	42.8	49.4
Tokyo	109.4	68.3	78	74	92.4	70.1
Singapore	n.a.	n.a.	n.a.	n.a.	n.a.	n.a.
New York	100.2	84.7	100	100	100	100

Date source: Website of UBS.

Note: The level of Zurich was taken as 100 in and before 2003 and the level of New York was taken as 100 in and after 2006.

2.2.2 Reputation and other factors

Reputation factors mainly include innovation, intellectual property, sustainable development, competitiveness and price level. We selected several indices in the top 30 listed in the GFCI rankings for comparison. As shown in table 2 - 8, China ranked high in global competitiveness and global city index, ranking 27th and 20th respectively out of the participating economies. But China lagged behind in both city momentum index and sustainable city index. China ranked 93rd out of 181 countries or regions in city momentum index, at a lower-middle level. It ranked 74th out of 100 participating countries or regions in sustainable city index, at a low level. This demonstrates China's fast competitiveness growth and urban development are not accompanied with green development and sustainable development.

Table 2 - 8 Comparison of Main Reputation Factors

Country/ Region	Global competitiveness		City momentum index		Sustainable city index		Global city index	
	Score in 2017	Ranking	Score in 2016	Ranking	Score in 2016	Ranking	Score in 2016	Ranking
Mainland China	5	27	63.35	93	47	74	30.4	20
UK	5.5	8	99.65	2	72	5	62.7	1
Hong Kong, China	5.5	6	77.2	39	67	16	44.2	5
Japan	5.5	9	85.12	12	59	45	46.7	4
Singapore	5.7	3	82.8	22	73	2	37.9	8
USA	5.9	2	100	1	62	26	62.5	2

Date sources: Website of World Economic Forum, website of IESE, website of Arcadis and website of ATKearney.

Note: A total of 137 countries or regions were involved in the global competitiveness ranking on a 100-point rating scale. A total of 181 countries or regions were involved in the city momentum index ranking on a 100-point rating scale. A total of 100 countries or regions were involved in the sustainable city index ranking on an 80-point rating scale. Only top 25 cities were listed for global city index.

Another important index of reputation and other factors is price level. The price level of a city determines the cost of its business operation, thus affecting the establishment of financial institutions, gathering of financial talents and other important indices of international financial centers. As shown in table 2 - 9, since 2006, the price level of New York was taken as 100, and the price level excluding rent of Shanghai has relatively increased by 30%, from 50.3% of that of New York in 2006 to 64.9% of that of New York in 2015. However, this level is still lower than those of London, Hong Kong and Tokyo, but the gap is narrowing. What's more, the price levels of the latter have been falling relative to that of New York over the past decade. As a result, the relative price level of Shanghai is gradually rising.

Table 2 - 9 Comparison of Price Level (excluding rent)

	2000	2003	2006	2009	2012	2015
Shanghai	86.3	69.7	50.3	64.1	56.2	64.9
London	94.8	97.6	110.6	84.6	87.2	84.7
Hong Kong	88.6	108.1	82.1	80.9	73.2	72.9
Tokyo	140.1	106.7	106.8	102	109	83.1
Singapore	n. a.	n. a.	n. a.	n. a.	n. a.	n. a.
New York	103.8	104.5	100	100	100	100

Data source: Website of UBS.

Note: The level of Zurich was taken as 100 in and before 2003 and the level of New York was taken as 100 in and after 2006.

The relative price levels including rents have changed more dramatically. As shown in table 2 - 10, the price level including rent of Shanghai was equivalent to 40% of that of New York in 2006, but the price level of Shanghai relative to New York rose to 54. 3% in 2015, increasing by 38%. Only Hong Kong experienced a slight increase of about 5% relative to the price level including rent of New York in the same period, while London and Tokyo saw a significant decline.

Table 2 - 10 Comparison of Price Level (including rent)

	2000	2003	2006	2009	2012	2015
Shanghai	89.8	71.9	39.3	48.9	49.7	54.3
London	110.2	111.4	105.5	69.9	83	79.5
Hong Kong	110.5	122.5	73	75.2	75.2	76.9
Tokyo	150.6	110.3	93.4	85.3	100.1	70.6
Singapore	n. a.	n. a.	n. a.	n. a.	n. a.	n. a.
New York	118.6	120.2	100	100	100	100

Data source: Website of UBS.

Note: The level of Zurich was taken as 100 in and before 2003 and the level of New York was taken as 100 in and after 2006.

In summary, China's overall indices are still lagging far behind those of other countries (regions) where the international financial centers are located in terms of reputation and other factors, and the gap between some indices of China and other countries (regions) is quite huge. In the comparison of city indices, the price level of Shanghai is still lower than that of other international financial centers, but it grows relatively fast, especially the rent level. This may become a factor restricting the construction of Shanghai International Financial Center in the future.

2.2.3 Infrastructure

Infrastructure factors include office building rent, real estate transparency, information communication technology development, road density, railway density, subway network length, environmental performance, traffic index, etc. Among them, the most relevant factor with the ranking of GFCI financial centers is the office building rent index.

As shown in table 2 - 11, the office building rent index of Pudong of Shanghai in December 2013 was USD 119.5 per square foot, ranking 12th in the world's major cities. At that time, the West End of London had the world's highest office building rent, up to USD 259.36 which was 116% higher than that of Shanghai. The office building rent in Central of Hong

Table 2 - 11 Comparison of Office Building Rent Index

City	Score in 2013	Ranking	Remark
Shanghai	119.5	12	Pudong
London	259.36	1	West End
Hong Kong	234.3	2	Central
Tokyo	154.67	8	Otemachi
Singapore	98.5	20	Downtown
New York	130.64	11	Manhattan

Date source: Website of CBRE.

Note: The rent per square foot is calculated in USD in December, 2013.

Kong ranked 2nd in the world, up to USD 234.3 per square foot. However, the office building rent of Shanghai is close to the USD 130. 64 of Manhattan of New York, higher than that of Downtown Singapore, which suggests that the office building rent of Shanghai is at a high level.

Among other major infrastructure indices, we list two factors of high correlation, namely network connectivity and road quality, as shown in table 2 - 12. Both factors are national (regional) data. As we can see, China ranked 59th out of 130 countries or regions in terms of network connectivity, at an upper middle level. China ranked 24th out of 140 countries or regions in terms of road quality. Considering that China is a vast country with great differences between the eastern and western regions, the overall road quality of China has reached a fairly good level, ranking even higher than that of the United States.

Table 2 - 12 Comparison of Other Major Infrastructure Indices

Country/Region	Network connectivity		Road quality	
	Score in 2016	Ranking	Score in 2016	Ranking
Mainland China	4.2	59	5.6	24
UK	5.7	8	6.3	8
Hong Kong, China	5.6	12	5.9	14
Japan	5.6	10	6.5	3
Singapore	6	1	5.7	20
USA	5.8	6	4.4	54

Date source: Website of World Economic Forum.

Note: A total of 130 countries or regions were involved in the network connectivity ranking on a 6-point rating scale. A total of 140 countries or regions were involved in the road quality ranking on a 6-point rating scale.

2.2.4 Human capital

Human capital indices include the number of graduate students in social science, visa restrictions index, human development index of the

United Nations, number of high net worth individuals, global skills index, global talent index, physical quality of life index, crime rate index etc., among which the global destination cities index and resident purchasing power index have high correlation with the rankings of GFCI international financial centers.

As shown in table 2 - 13, the number of international tourists traveling to Shanghai in 2016 is 6,904,000, ranking 25th in major cities around the world. During the same period, Hong Kong ranked 1st in the world with 26,552,000 international tourists, London ranked 3rd with 19,190,000, Singapore ranked 4th with 16,604,000 and New York ranked 8th with 12,650,000. There is still plenty of room for Shanghai to attract international tourists.

Table 2 - 13 Comparison of Global Destination

City	Person-time in 2016	Ranking
Shanghai	6,904	25
London	19,190	3
Hong Kong	26,552	1
Tokyo	9,272	13
Singapore	16,604	4
New York	12,650	8

Data source: Website of Euromonitor
Note: The unit is 1000 person-time.

Resident purchasing power is also an important index of human resource factors. As shown in table 2 - 14, the purchasing power of Shanghai residents has increased significantly since 2000 from 10.9% of the New York level in 2000 to 32.9% of the New York level in 2015, almost doubling. But as a city of the developing country, the purchasing power of Shanghai residents is still far behind those of other international financial centers such as New York. The purchasing power of Shanghai residents in 2015 is about one-third of that of Hong Kong, 37% of that of Tokyo and 41% of that of London.

Table 2 – 14 Comparison of Resident Purchasing Power

	2000	2003	2006	2009	2012	2015
Shanghai	10.2	19.1	26.7	24.7	36.6	32.9
London	70.4	65.5	84	76.9	73.1	80.4
Hong Kong	64.9	42	50.5	58.1	72.6	99.3
Tokyo	86.2	74.7	87.6	82.2	80.9	89
Singapore	n.a.	n.a.	n.a.	n.a.	n.a.	n.a.
New York	93.6	75.2	100	100	100	100

Date source: Website of UBS.

Note: The level of Zurich was taken as 100 in and before 2003 and the level of New York was taken as 100 in and after 2006.

If residents' cost of living is taken into account, the actual purchasing power of Shanghai residents is further below those of the other five financial centers. As shown in table 2 – 15, where the level of New York is taken as 100, the cost of living in Shanghai was 56.16 in 2017, ranking 339th out of 540 cities in the world. Since the purchasing power of Shanghai residents is less than one-third of that of New York, but the cost of living is more than half that of New York, the actual purchasing power of Shanghai residents is lower than that given in table 2 – 13. Therefore, control of the rapid rise of price level and living cost is of great importance for building Shanghai into an international financial center.

Table 2 – 15 Comparison of Residents' Cost of Living in 2017

	Cost of living	Rent	Cost of living plus rent	Grocery price	Restaurant price	Local purchasing power index	Ranking in 540 cities
Shanghai	56.16	41.95	49.3	61.7	40.74	66.16	339
London	88.69	76.67	82.89	67.36	96.36	92.61	42

(续表)

	Cost of living	Rent	Cost of living plus rent	Grocery price	Restaurant price	Local purchasing power index	Ranking in 540 cities
Hong Kong	78.72	79.54	79.12	83.47	56.17	82.86	132
Tokyo	93.81	37.07	66.45	99.67	58.93	106.42	21
Singapore	91.4	71.89	81.99	83.64	64.4	95.89	29
New York	100	100	100	100	100	100	14

Data source: Website of Mercer.
Note: The level of New York is taken as 100.

2.2.5 Financial sector development

Finally, we will analyze the financial sector development indices. As stated earlier, these indices are not listed in the 30 indices having the highest correlation with the results in the GFCI - 22 assessment. But as they serve as basic indices for international financial centers, their significance should not be underestimated.

There are many assessment indices for financial sector development, such as trading volume, volume of holding, volume of issuance and other data of products with various maturity and risk structures in capital market, money market, derivative product market, foreign exchange market and other kinds of financial markets. According to the needs of research, our analysis focuses on 15 indices used in the GFCI assessment, including transaction value of securities market, net assets of open-end funds, bank's net external positions and other financial market indices as well as comprehensive indices such as global connectivity index and liner shipping connectivity index.

As shown in table 2 - 16, the total capital market capitalization of Shanghai was USD 5.08 trillion by the end of 2017, higher than USD 4.35 trillion of Hong Kong market and USD 0.79 trillion of Singapore market and lower than USD 6.22 trillion of Tokyo market. But the gap between Shanghai market and New York market is wide. By the end of 2017, the total market capitalization of the two financial markets (NYSE and NASDAQ) in New York reached USD 22.08 trillion, almost as much as the sum of capitalization of Shanghai and Hong Kong, Tokyo and Singapore markets.

Table 2 - 16 Total Capital Market Capitalization

City	Total capitalization by the end of 2017	Transaction market	Remark
Shanghai	5,084,357.8	1.486,554,02	Shanghai Stock Exchange
London	n.a.	n.a.	
Hong Kong	4,350,500.7	0.450,251,715	Hong Kong Exchanges and Clearing Limited (HKEx)
Tokyo	6,222,834.7	0.932,807,874	Japan Exchange Group (JEG)
Singapore	787,279.5	0.270,072,085	Singapore Exchange Limited (SGX)
New York	22,081,367.0	1.171,650,74	Sum of New York Stock Exchange (NYSE) and National Association of Securities Dealers Automated Quotations (NASDAQ)

Data source: Website of World Federation of Exchanges.
Note: The unit is USD million.

From the perspective of trading volume of the capital market, as shown in table 2 - 17, the trading on Shanghai market is active. Its total value of transactions reached USD 7.56 trillion in 2017, higher than those of Tokyo, Hong Kong and Singapore markets, and equivalent to almost one-third of the total value of transactions of USD 25.87 trillion of two New York markets. If the market trading volume and total market value are compared, as shown in table 2 - 15, the trading on Shanghai market is the most active, with the ratio of trading volume to total market value reaching 1.48 which is not only much higher than those of Tokyo, Hong

Kong and Singapore markets but also considerably higher than that of New York market. This indicates that the speculative trading on Shanghai's capital market still accounts for a considerable proportion. A further analysis of the participant structure of each market reveals that there are a large number of retail investors on Shanghai's capital market, while on other capital markets the proportion of institutional investors is relatively high.

Table 2 - 17 Total Value of Capital Market Transactions

City	Total value of transactions	Domestic companies	Foreign companies	Remark
Shanghai	7,558,172.5	7,558,172.5	n.a.	Shanghai Stock Exchange
London	n.a.	n.a.	n.a.	
Hong Kong	1,958,820.4	1,892,862.2	65,958.2	HKEx
Tokyo	5,804,709.2	5,803,728.5	980.7	JEG
Singapore	212,622.2	212,622.2	n.a.	SGX
New York	25,871,650.0	23,370,990.0	2,500,660.0	Sum of NYSE and NASDAQ

Date source: Website of World Federation of Exchanges.

Note: The unit is USD million.

Table 2 - 18 shows another important financial development index used in the GFCI assessment, namely the proportion of bank credit to GDP. After the global financial crisis in 2008, each country began to take measures to stimulate economic growth. As a result, the proportion of bank credit to GDP in 2010 was relatively high except Singapore. During the period from 2010 to 2016, China's proportion of bank credit to GDP increased further, from 142.2% to 215%, indicating that China has not significantly reduced its economic growth's dependence on credit. During this period, the bank credit-to-GDP proportion of the USA, Japan and Hong Kong SAR grew at a modest rate, while the UK experienced a sustained decline. Only Singapore's bank credit-to-GDP proportion continued to rise.

Table 2 - 18 Proportion of Bank Credit to GDP (%)

	2010	2011	2012	2013	2014	2015	2016
Mainland China	142.2	140.6	149.1	155.7	167.2	193.4	215.0
UK	206.2	197.2	192.2	180.0	166.9	161.1	165.8
Hong Kong, China	195.4	207.1	201.1	222.6	236.0	211.9	210.6
Japan	313.8	323.0	330.0	338.1	345.7	341.8	345.1
Singapore	80.8	88.2	95.2	110.9	126.2	119.4	135.1
USA	231.4	231.0	233.5	247.5	250.6	236.0	241.9

Date source: Website of the World Bank.

Table 2 - 19 involves the global connectivity index used in the GFCI assessment. From the period from 2005 to 2015, China scored 48 in terms of global connectivity, while it fell from 57 to 68 slowly in the world rankings, which indicates that China's progress in the global connectivity is slower than other economies around the world. Of the other five financial centers, Singapore has the highest global connectivity, basically keeping 2nd place in the world, and the UK ranked 8th.

Table 2 - 19 Comparison of Global Connectivity

	2005		2007		2009		2011		2013		2015	
	Score	Ranking	Score	Ranking	Score	Ranking	Score	Ranking	Score	Ranking	Score	Ranking
Mainland China	46	57	47	58	45	62	48	59	48	65	48	68
UK	77	6	78	8	78	7	79	5	78	7	75	8
Hong Kong, China	70	14	69	18	68	15	69	16	70	17	69	17
Japan	52	40	56	39	53	45	55	43	57	39	59	38
Singapore	84	3	85	3	83	2	84	2	85	2	87	2
USA	59	29	62	28	63	25	64	27	64	27	64	27

Date source: Website of DHL

Note: The perfect score is 100.

Table 2 - 20 lists the liner shipping connectivity index used in the

GFCI assessment. China is at a high level in terms of this index, not only higher those of Hong Kong SAR and Singapore, but also much higher than those of the USA, the UK and Japan. This may be the result of China's world-leading imports and exports of goods, and it is one of the few indices in which China took the lead on the whole among the more than 100 factors used in the GFCI assessment.

Table 2 - 20 Liner Shipping Connectivity Index

	2010	2011	2012	2013	2014	2015	2016
Mainland China	143.57	152.06	156.19	157.51	165.05	167.13	167.48
UK	87.53	87.46	84	87.72	87.95	95.22	97.23
Hong Kong, China	113.6	115.27	117.18	116.63	115.99	116.76	101.02
Japan	67.43	67.81	63.09	65.68	62.14	68.82	78.9
Singapore	103.76	105.02	113.16	106.91	113.16	117.13	122.7
USA	83.8	81.63	91.7	92.8	95.09	96.74	98.7

Data source: Website of the World Bank.
Note: The highest score is 100 in 2004.

2.3 Analysis of Gag between Shanghai and Major Leading International Financial Centers

Based on the above benchmarking analysis of the main factors used in the assessment of GFCI financial centers, the gap between Shanghai and major international financial centers such as New York can be summarized as follows.

First of all, there is a clear gap between Shanghai and other international financial centers when indices are accessed for the countries (regions) where the financial centers are located, and Shanghai takes the lead only in terms of a few indices. Nearly half of the objective factors in the GFCI assessment are indices at national (regional) level obtained through various channels, such as the corruption perceptions index and government efficiency index. Shanghai as a financial center in the top 20 cities is one of the few cities from developing countries (regions) and only China's overall assessment data in these aspects can be used, thus widening the gap between the assessment results of Shanghai and international financial center cities such as New York.

Secondly, in comparison of relevant indices of Shanghai and other international financial center cities, the overall gap is not huge, but the structural gap is prominent. During the GFCI assessment, about the other half of objective factors are various data at city level, such as trading volume of financial market, rent level of office buildings, purchasing power of urban residents, price level of cities, number of foreign tourists attracted to the cities, etc. In respect of these city-level indices, Shanghai is roughly comparable with the other five international financial center cities, and even has a comparative advantage in terms of several indices. At the city level, the gap between Shanghai and other major international financial center cities is mainly manifested as: first, its internationalization level is low. For example, the total market value of listed companies on the Shanghai Stock Exchange exceeds that on the HKEx, but no foreign companies has been listed for transactions here so far. Second, its degree of openness is low. Shanghai, for example, has far more visa restrictions for scientific and financial talents than Hong Kong and Singapore. Third, Shanghai's overall reputation and attractiveness need to be improved. For example, compared with other international metropolises, Shanghai still has obvious deficiencies in the convenience of urban rail transit, sufficiency of barrier-free facilities, etc.

In view of the above deficiencies and insufficiencies, in order to further improve the level of Shanghai International Financial Center, lots of efforts should be devoted to improving Shanghai's urban function. And

Shanghai should be benchmarked against the two top international financial centers New York and London, and other major financial centers including Hong Kong of China, Singapore and Tokyo so as to keep up with the international advanced benchmarks in such aspects as legal environment, government efficiency, business environment and price stability.

References

(I) Singapore strengthens its position as an international financial center

In the face of the intensifying global economic competition and pervasive impact of disruptive technologies, Singapore government has recently announced the Industry Transformation Map (ITM) for financial service in order to strengthen Singapore's position as a financial center, and create more high-quality jobs.

Singapore seeks to become a leading global financial center in Asia. By virtue of the ITM, the government aims to achieve an average annual growth of 4.3% in financial service sector, nearly twice as high as the overall economic growth rate and 2.4% growth in productivity. In addition, the ITM is expected to create 4,000 jobs annually.

Singapore government said ITM was "ambitious" in such an era of dramatic changes in the financial sector; The government was determined to make Singapore the ultimate winner and ensured that the financial sector would continue to be the main pillar of future economic growth.

Singapore is the world's third-largest financial center, after London and New York. Singapore's financial sector has already accumulated a lot of experience in foreign exchange trading and wealth management. Presently, the output value of financial service sector, which provides 154,000 jobs, accounts for about 12% of Singapore's GDP. Additionally, the rapid regional economic development and great demand for infrastructure construction have created favorable conditions for the development of Singapore's financial sector. Almost half of Singapore's direct foreign investments have been made in finance and insurance. The influx of foreign banks has also brought in many financial talents. On the other hand, the development of wealth management has attracted a lot of funds to Singapore.

The depth and breadth of Singapore's financial market have strengthened its role as a financial intermediary in the region. When China was internationalizing its currency, Singapore became the main RMB clearing center outside China. China's current "Belt and Road Initiative" has also brought business opportunities for Singapore's financial sector.

The ITM emphasizes the importance of financial innovation and encourages existing entrepreneurs to compete and cooperate with financial technology innovators. Singapore has established sound infrastructures and an ecological system in the financial sector and is in a position to meet the challenges of financial technology. Currently, more than 20 foreign financial institutions have set up financial technology laboratories or research centers in Singapore. More than 400 financial technology start-ups have become a part of its financial ecosystem.

(II) Hong Kong's financial sector is facing new opportunities

In the face of new opportunities for the development of Guangdong-Hong Kong-Macao Greater Bay Area, the financial circles generally believe that if Hong Kong could coordinate with Macao, Qianhai, Hengqin and Nansha on the financial development, and better adapt to the new financing demand of new economic development, not only the economic development of the entire Greater Bay Area will be strongly promoted, but its own position as an international financial center could also be consolidated.

1) Advantages

As an important financial center in the world, Hong Kong has many irreplaceable advantages as it has always served as main listing and financing platform for mainland enterprises' "going global" and is also the main channel for internationalization of RMB and two-way opening up of the mainland capital market. Zhuang Tailiang, executive director of Lau Chor Tak Institute of Global Economics and Finance, the Chinese University of Hong Kong, believes that Hong Kong can become the financial center of Greater Bay Area as it boasts free flow of funds, rich financial talents, highly developed information, low tax rate, and a good English environment.

Recent years witness the rapid development of Internet economy, artificial intelligence, big data, biotechnology, and other forms of new economy, which has become an important engine for the economic growth of Greater Bay Area and even the whole China, and also presents new demands for Hong Kong's financial sector development. Faced with new challenges, Carrie Lam, Chief Executive of Hong Kong SAR said that Hong Kong could assist and promote the "going global" of Greater Bay Area cities in such aspects as international asset management, fund management, risk management, project financing, green finance and financial technology. Hong Kong will promote the financial services and capital flow by strengthening financial cooperation with the mainland, strive to promote the innovation and development of the Greater Bay Area, and provide required financial service supports for the "Belt and Road Initiative" project.

2) Innovative thinking

With reference to the financial system innovation, in the face of new economic industry development of Greater Bay Area, Hong Kong badly needs further improvement of the listing platform architecture and creation of new business models and systems to meet the needs of new economic development as it is beneficial to Hong Kong's progress and also can better serve the Greater Bay Area.

In June 2017, HKEx released listing framework consultation documents, suggesting establishing an innovation board which is divided into "main innovation board" and "initial innovation board", both of which allow dual-class share structure. The innovation board proposed by HKEx, especially the "initial innovation board", caters precisely to the needs of new economic industries in the Greater Bay Area and will offer assistance in financing of these enterprises.

At present, the quantity of new economic industries in Hong Kong market is not large, but that is large in the Greater Bay Area. Many international investors are interested in new economic industries and can be attracted through Hong Kong to invest in such projects in the environments, laws and regulatory systems which they are familiar with. In the future, the development of HKEx's innovation board must rely on projects in the Greater Bay Area.

3) Embracing the opportunities

As an international financial center, Hong Kong has open financial system and business network extending around the world. The stronger economy of the Greater Bay Area will bring more opportunities for Hong Kong's finance and professional services and contributes to consolidation of the position of Hong Kong as an international financial center. The financial cooperation between Hong Kong and various cities in the Greater Bay Area will not only provide financial support for the development of Greater Bay Area, but also can realize the development of Hong Kong.

Although Hong Kong, as a traditional international financial center, has significant advantages and rich experience, it also has certain disadvantages. The living costs in Hong Kong are high and it is faced with the pressure of financial brain drain. But when Hong Kong-Zhuhai-Macao Bridge and Guangzhou-Shenzhen-Hong Kong Express Rail Link Hong Kong section are open to traffic in succession, the traffic will be more and more convenient. If the Greater Bay Area can provide cheap housing, we believe that the pressure in this respect facing Hong Kong will get eased. However, in the face of competition from emerging financial markets such as Macao, Qianhai, Hengqin and Nansha, to coordinate development and jointly build a financial core circle out of the Greater Bay Area will become a major challenge in the future.

Chapter III

Analysis of Construction Trend of Shanghai International Financial Center

3.1 New Historical Development Opportunity in New Era

According to the 19th National Congress of the Communist Party of China, socialism with Chinese characteristics has entered a new era. This new era has higher requirements on the construction of Shanghai International Financial Center. In this context, Shanghai Municipal proposes a new target of "basically build up an international financial center suited to our country's economic strength and the international position of RMB and join the rank of the global financial center". To achieve this new target, construction of Shanghai International Financial Center should, with serving real economy as original intention and preventing financial risk as bottom line, follow President Xi Jinping's ideas on socialism with Chinese characteristics in the new era to proactively serve national strategies, strengthen the linkage with construction of the pilot free trade zone, science and technology innovation center and "Belt and Road Initiative" and continuously improve the influence and radiation of Shanghai International Financial Center.

3.1.1 Strengthening the linkage with achievement of higher-quality integrated development of Yangtze River Delta Area

The Party Central Committee and State Council attach great importance to the integrated development of Yangtze River Delta Area. General Secretary Xi Jinping has given important instructions for several times and recently he gave important instructions again in the *Report on Promoting the Integrated Development of Yangtze River Delta Area*, pointing out that "we should push the Yangtze River Delta Area forward to achieve higher-quality integrated development so as to better lead the development of Yangtze River Economic Belt and better serve the overall national development". The important instructions given by General Secretary Xi Jinping this time are of great significance and can give importance guidance on promotion of the integrated development of Yangtze River Delta Area. Shanghai should play a leading role and take the international financial center building as an opportunity to set a good example in promoting the higher-quality integrated development of Yangtze River Delta Area by: ① constantly pushing the Yangtze River Delta Area forward to achieve higher-quality integrated development; ② innovating and implementing the regional cooperation mechanisms and promoting the substantive breakthroughs in key areas; and ③ focusing on the overall situation, serving the whole situation, and precisely determining the work linking points and focuses. Shanghai should take the initiative to integrate into the integrated development of Yangtze River Delta Area to make greater contribution to the overall national development.

3.1.2 To Strengthen the linkage with the financial reform of the free trade zone—a new breakthrough point

New deployment has been made for the construction of the pilot free trade zone in a new era at the 19th National Congress of the Communist

Party of China—"granting the pilot free trade zone more autonomy in reform for exploring on the construction of the free trade port". The free trade port is a special economic function zone with the highest degree of opening-up currently around the world which may inject new power to the construction of China (Shanghai) Pilot Free Trade Zone, and a new breakthrough point to further advance the financial reform in Shanghai and the construction of Shanghai International Financial Center. The free trade port adopts the institutional system of "release of the first line, safe and efficient control over the second line" and inevitably demands more open finance and more convenient cross-border financial activities.

3.1.3 To strengthen the linkage with the construction of the science and technology innovation center—serving real economy as original intention

As is emphasized at the 19th National Congress of the Communist Party of China, "innovation is the most powerful lever for development". Shanghai is accelerating the construction of a science and technology innovation center with global influence. The new era grants innovation higher significance for the construction of a modern economic system. In the new era, the construction of Shanghai International Financial Center must firmly stick to its original intention of serving real economy, follow new development concepts and strengthen the linkage with the construction of Shanghai Technology Innovation Center, so as to provide good financial service for high-quality development of Shanghai and even the whole country.

3.1.4 To strengthen the linkage with "Belt and Road Initiative" construction

As is required by General Secretary Xi Jinping, "China (Shanghai)

Pilot Free Trade Zone should be a bridgehead serving the construction of the Belt and Road Initiative and facilitating market players to go global". Shanghai International Financial Center must strongly support and serve the "Belt and Road Initiative" construction and become the bridgehead for providing financial service for "Belt and Road Initiative". Shanghai municipal government has formulated and issued *Shanghai's Action Plan for Playing the Role of Bridgehead in "Belt and Road Initiative" Construction*. In accordance with the deployment of the action plan, financial institutions in Shanghai are strengthening the linkage with "Belt and Road Initiative" construction, actively docking the financial service demand of "Belt and Road Initiative" construction, making innovation in products and service and enhancing financial support for "Belt and Road Initiative" construction and "Go Global" strategy by providing all-around cross-border financial service.

3.1.5 To firmly hold the bottom line of non-occurrence of systematic financial risks—strengthening financial regulation as emphasis

As is emphasized at the 19th National Congress of the Communist Party of China, we should "refine the financial regulatory system and hold the bottom line of non-occurrence of systematic financial risks". Numerous financial institutions, rapid development of internet finance and frequent cross-border financial activities have surely brought Shanghai potential financial risks that cannot be ignored; with developed financial market and increasing cross-market financial products and business, Shanghai will also face such financial risks as bond default that occur in other regions of China. Therefore, the task for Shanghai to prevent financial risks is tougher; Shanghai should put focus on refining the financial regulatory system, carrying out campaigns against financial risks and optimizing the financial development environment, to safeguard the bottom line of financial risks with both short-term plans and long-term plans.

3.2 Global Political Change and Development and Trend of Economy and Trade

At present, global economic recovery gradually gets stabilized and the world economy is at a stage of collaborative growth where major economies present a collective growth again after 10 years, putting an end to the growth stagnation after the Great Recession.

3.2.1 Development review of 2017

In 2017, the word economy went through a period of transformation from shrinkage to sluggish recovery. First, the driving power for growth of global trade has increased. The World Trade Organization has increased the global trade growth of 2017 by 1.2% to 3.6%. Second, the global employment situation is tending to a good prospect. The unemployment rate of America, Eurozone and Japan has fallen to a record low in recent years. Third, the global inflation has gradually risen back. The inflation rate of America, Eurozone and Japan has risen by different degrees. Fourth, the global manufacturing has recovered orderly. IMF has continuously upregulated the global economic growth expectation of 2017 to 3.6%, increasing by 0.5% based on the first upregulation to 3.1% in 2016. The Organization for Economic Co-operation and Development and the World Bank have also increased the global economic growth expectation of 2017 to 3.5% and 2.7% respectively. Fifth, the monetary policies of major economies have gradually converged. The Federal Reserve Board raised interest rates for the fifth time in Dec. 2017; the Bank of England raised interest rates in Nov. 2017 for the first time over the last 10 years; Canada raised interest rates twice in Jul. and Sep. 2017 successively; on Nov. 30, 2017, the Bank of Korea announced to raise benchmark interest rates by 25 base points from 1.25% to 1.50%, the first time since Jun. 2011.

3.2.2 Predictive analysis of 2018

In 2018, uncertainty factors will still exist in the international economic and financial market. First, the global economy has not yet got rid of dependence on high growth and slack policy of credit and loan. Excessively loose currency environment at earlier stage has led to a serious phenomenon of "shift from real economy to virtual economy", thus breeding asset bubble and accumulating great financial risks. Second, some developed economies are gradually quitting unconventional currency policies. For example, America is implementing gradual interest rate hike and gradual balance-sheet reduction and the European Central Bank is also gradually scaling back its bond-buying program, which will lead to earlier appearance of the inflection point of global liquidity and intensified capital outflow of emerging markets. Third, 2018 is the year of "political re-election" and therefore, Black Swan event as well as chain reaction should be avoided. The year of 2018 will witness the mid-term election of America and presidential election of Russia. Obvious contradictions concerning geopolitics, religion, nationality and terrorism still exist in the Middle East; Brexit has triggered turbulence to global financial market; and the Sade event has influenced Korea's foreign trade with other countries. Fourth, the structural reform of major countries is faced with high uncertainty. Trump's "America First" and tax reform has led to an increase in deficit by USD 1 trillion and capital construction and other policies has caused an impact on international industrial division and cross-border capital flow; "Abeconomics" of Japan is confronted with such restrictions as heavy debt burden and aging population; and "Modi's reform" of India is also confronted with great resistance.

In particular, a new round of conflict has been caused to Sino-US trade. Trump's government takes more radical trade measures in 2018, which will cause great and profound influence upon China, America's allies and partners and America itself. The trade disputes between China and America have confronted the World Trade Organization with threat. The biggest problem so far is whether China and America are willing to settle disputes and ease tensions through the World Trade Organization. China and America have entered the era of "competitive cooperation". Sino-American cooperation will bring significant economic and political benefits to both sides. China and America should, based on the principle of complementary advantages, mutual benefit and win and moderate economic benefit, establish mechanisms, channels and platforms to realize new increase in economic trade between China and America.

It is predicted that the global economy will keep recovering in 2018. The International Monetary Fund, the Organization for Economic Co-operation and Development and the World Bank have raised economic growth of 2018 by 0.1%, 0.2% and 0.2% based on that of 2017 to 3.7%, 3.7% and 2.9% respectively. As for monetary policy, America, Japan, Britain, the European Central Bank and other economies will have the same or mostly the same trend of monetary policy and keep providing forward guidance.

3.3 Economic and Financial Situation and Trend of China

Steady progress of economic development since the 18th National Congress of the Communist Party of China continued in the year of 2017. From 2018, in the context of different progress of economic recovery in different regions around the world and tough and complex international situation, China's economy increases at its own rhythm and the economic index continues improving. It is predicted that in 2018, China will still be confronted with a complex external environment with increasing uncertainty and instability and an internal environment with coexistence of opportunities and challenges.

3.3.1 Development review of 2017

After the financial crisis, China's financial market has recovered at a steady pace, but it is still somewhat sensitive and vulnerable. In 2017, China's economic growth was stable on the whole; the economic structure was optimized continuously; the contribution of the service industry to economic growth kept increasing; consumer demand was still the main driving force for economic growth; new driving forces became important power for economic growth; and the quality of economic growth improved constantly. With the change in the trend of monetary policy of global financial market in 2017, the tendency of capital reflow to developed economies was obvious, causing a prominent influence upon the liquidity of developing countries including China. In particular, the liquidity of domestic financial market would tighten under the effect of adjustments in macro policies at the end of the quarter and the year and in the season when funds are conventionally handed over to the state treasury. This situation spread to stock market, bond market and commodity market and presented a certain transmission effect, thus influencing the profits of financial institutions and significantly increasing the financing cost of real economy. Besides, under greater spillover effect of international financial crisis and the effect of cyclical and structural factors of domestic economy, "gray rhino" risks, including shadow banking, non-performing loan, enterprise bond, internet finance, real estate bubble, local implicit debt and illegal fund-raising, were formed in the current financial field and systematic financial risks were caused by cross-market, product and institution correlation to the financial market.

3.3.2 Predictive analysis of 2018

As was proposed in the reports of the 19th National Congress of the Communist Party of China, "China's economy has been transitioning from a phase of rapid growth to a stage of high-quality development". In 2018, China's development has come to a new starting point, emphasizing more on quality, efficiency, fairness and sustainability and committed to gradually solving some prominent problems such as unbalanced and insufficient development. On Mar. 5, Premier Li Keqiang presented a report on the work of the government at the Thirteenth National People's Congress, emphasizing promoting progress while maintaining stability, realizing high-quality development, pursuing supply-side structural reform as main task and working hard for better quality, higher efficiency, and more robust drivers of economic growth through reform. The main development targets for 2018 are as follows: GDP growth of around 6.5%; CPI increase of around 3%; over 11 million new urban jobs; basic parity in personal income growth and economic growth; a steady rise in import and export volumes, and a basic equilibrium in the balance of payments; a drop of at least 3% in energy consumption per unit of GDP, and continued reductions in the release of major pollutants; substantive progress in supply-side structural reform, basically stable macro leverage, and systematic and effective prevention and control of risk, etc. Though the supply-side structural reform currently in effect has made some achievements, such reform in the future will face increasing difficulties and enter a most critical stage.

As for cutting overcapacity, the exit of backward production capacities basically finished and the rebound in prices of upstream products have an influence on the willingness of enterprises to cut overcapacity; as for releasing new capacity, there is still room for improvement in the production quality and benefit of enterprises and the level of social innovation and entrepreneurship. As for deleveraging, reducing the government's liabilities involves reform of financial system, thus making it more difficult to guard against financial risks. As for cutting excess inventory, the pressure remains in the commercial real asset and the housing inventory of some third and fourth-tier cities and counties. Long-effect mechanism and basic system for steady and healthy development of the real estate market have not been established yet and the housing rental market has been developing slowly. As for reducing costs, the development of real economy is confronted with lack of vitality due to the restriction of high institutional trade cost and it becomes more difficult to realize reform of social welfare system, logistics system and tax system in the short run. As for strengthening points of weakness, eco-environmental protection remains a long and arduous task, and lack of innovation in poverty alleviation, urban and rural development, employment, education, medical treatment, housing, pension and other areas concerning people's livelihood influences the increase in effective supply and restricts the development of people's livelihood. "Belt and Road Initiative" business and other international businesses are still faced with prominent risks.

3.4 Impact of China's Economy on the World

In 2017, the growth of China's economy rose back to 6.9%, maintaining its leading position around the world. According to the estimation of the World Bank, the growth of the world economy in 2017 was around 3%. Calculated on this basis, China's economy increased its proportion in the world economy to around 15. 3% in 2017, with a contribution rate of around 34% to the growth of world economy.

"Steady rise of China's economy has forcefully advanced the recovery of world economy, promoted the development of world trade and brought unprecedented development opportunities to people all over the world. The speech of President Xi Jinping at the opening ceremony of the Bo'ao Forum for Asia identified a series of major initiatives for China's further opening-up, which means China will bring more benefits to the world."

3.4.1 China's economy still being major impetus for the growth of world economy

In recent years, China's economy has kept growing at a medium-high speed and become an indispensable engine for the recovery and sustainable development of global economy. From 2013 to 2016, the proportion of China's GDP in the world's economic aggregate, which is calculated at the exchange rate of each year, increased by 2.3% from 12.5% to 14.8%. As is calculated at the fixed dollar value in 2010, China realized an average economic growth of 7.2% during the 4 years, far higher than that of the three major developed economies, i. e. America (2. 1%), Eurozone (1.2%) and Japan (1. 1%), forcefully driving the growth of world economy with an average contribution rate of over 30%.

As the world's second largest economic entity, China's steady economic growth has played an essential role in reducing the risk of fluctuation in world economy. From 2013 to 2016, the fluctuation range of China's economic growth was only 1. 1%, obviously lower than that of America's, Eurozone's and Japan's in the same period. The result shows that if the impact of China's economy is not taken into account, the average growth of world economy from 2013 to 2016 will decrease by 0.6% while the fluctuation intensity will increase by 5.2%.

3.4.2 Chinese market being key power for the growth of world consumption

China has nearly 1/5 of the world's population. With its people on the way to achieve an all-round well-to-do society, China has become a consumption market with the highest growth and the largest potential around the world.

In the last few years, China's final consumption has presented the world's highest average annual rate of contribution to the growth of world consumption. Calculated at the fixed dollar price, the average annual rate of contribution of China's final consumption to the growth of world consumption from 2013 to 2016 was 23.4%, that of America's, Eurozone's and Japan's in the same period being 23%, 7.9% and 2.1% respectively; the average growth of China's final consumption was 7.5%, that of America's, Eurozone's and Japan's in the same period being 2.2%, 1% and 0.6% respectively, the average annual growth of the world's consumption market was 2.4%.

China has been the world's largest source country of outbound tourists for years in a row. According to statistics from related departments, outbound tourists from China reached 130 million person-times, an increase of 7% over the previous year and their expenditures for international tourism were USD 115.29 billion, an increase of 5%. Official statistics also show that Chinese tourists spent USD 13 thousand per capita in America in 2016 and their tourism expenditure reached USD 35.22 billion in the same year, bringing an average of around USD 97 million to America every day.

3.4.3 China's import trade being significant force for rebalancing world economy

In recent years, China's import demand has been rapidly expanded, making increasingly more contributions to the prosperity of international trade and effectively promoting rebalancing of the world economy. According to the statistics of the World Bank, the proportion of the total amount of China's import goods and service in the global import market rose by 1.3% from 8.4% to 9.7% in 2011 - 2016 while that of America, Eurozone and Japan's dropped by 0.4% in the same period.

In 2017, China's import continued growing steadily, making a higher contribution to the growth of world trade. According to the statistics of the World Trade Organization, China's import growth was 10.4%,8.1%, 7.6% and 6.5% higher than America's, German's, Japan's and the world's respectively in Jan. -Oct. 2017; in the first three quarters of 2017, the rate of contribution of China's import growth to the world's reached 17% and the proportion of China's import in the world's increased to 10.2%.

China is also an important bulk commodity importer. In 2017, China renewed a record in export of crude oil, iron ores and soybeans which reached 420 million, 1.075 billion and 95.54 million tons and rose by 5%, 10.1% and 13.9% from the previous year respectively, with an increase in average price of 29.6%, 28.65 and 5% respectively, thus playing an important role in stabilizing the price of bulk commodities and advancing the economic recovery of raw material exporting countries.

President Xi Jinping announced at the Bo'ao Forum for Asia in Mar. 2018 that China would hold the first China International Import Expo in Shanghai in Nov. 2018. On May 19, Liu He, the special envoy of President Xi Jinping, a member of the Communist Party's Politburo, Vice Premier of the State Council and the Chinese leader of the China-America Comprehensive Economic Dialogue, stressed that China has an enormous moderate-income group and will become the world's largest market. If any exporting country wishes to gain a share in the Chinese market which is highly competitive, it must improve the competitiveness of its products and services and make Chinese people willing to buy them. Chinese people are willing to buy things not only from America, but from all over the world.

3.4.4 China's reform and opening-up providing new important opportunities for the world

China's development not only brings benefits to Chinese people, but creates development opportunities for all developing and developed countries. The "Belt and Road Initiative" proposed by China has received active response from numerous countries. At present, more than 100 countries and international organizations have participated in the "Belt and Road Initiative" construction and over 80 of them have signed a cooperation agreement with China.

In 2017, Chinese enterprises made non-financial direct investment in 59 countries along the "Belt and Road Initiative", signed new foreign project contracts with total amount of USD 144.32 billion, a year-on-year increase of 14.5%, and realized turnover of USD 85.53 billion, a year-on-year increase of 12.6%.

China's huge demand on services and high-tech products provides developed countries with unprecedented cooperation opportunities. According to the statistical data of United States Department of Commerce, export of goods and services to China created 910 thousand employment positions for America in 2015. China's huge population scale and steady economic growth provide development space for enterprises from all over the world. More and more enterprises of developed countries have entered the Chinese market, strengthened cooperation with China and gained generous profits.

"China will not close its door to the world; we will only become more and more open", President Xi Jinping's speech at the Bo'ao Forum for Asia clearly expressed China's standpoint. As a responsible world power, China will stay committed to openness, connectivity and mutual benefits, contribute to the establishment of a community with a shared future for mankind, promote common prosperity and development in today's world, and bring more and more development opportunities for other countries all over the world.

3.5 Analysis of Construction Trend of Shanghai International Financial Center in 2018

At present, Shanghai has become an international financial center city with the highest concentration of domestic and foreign financial institutions, the most complete financial factor market and the strongest financial service capacity and radiation function in China, and the first choice for domestic and foreign financial talents and institutions to seek development in China. According to the requirements of Shanghai's 13th Five Year Plan, Shanghai will basically build up an international financial center suited to our country's economic strength and the international position of RMB and join the rank of the global financial center by 2020. To achieve the planning target on schedule, it is of great significance to predict and analyze the construction trend of Shanghai International Financial Center in 2018.

3.5.1 Improving the efficiency of financial service

According to the reports of the 19th National Congress of the Communist Party of China, the principal contradiction facing Chinese society in the new era is that between unbalanced and inadequate development and the people's ever-growing needs for a better life. In industrial structure, the contradiction manifests as unbalanced and inadequate development of the service industry, especially of the modern service industry, relative to the manufacturing industry. In demand structure, it manifests as unbalanced and inadequate consumption relative to investment. From the view of growth momentum, the pivotal role of innovation has not played in a balanced and adequate way. In the process of construction of Shanghai International Financial Center, the focus of the finance sector should transfer from conventional industry to modern service industry and advanced manufacturing industry, from the service mainly for producers to that more for customers, and from the extensive financial development pattern of mobilizing savings and promoting large-scale investment to the intensive pattern of utilizing financial technologies and allocating financial resources in an efficient way, thus practically improving the efficiency of financial service.

3.5.2 Building a stable financial system

As the core of modern economy, finance plays an important role in accelerating adjustment of economic structure, supporting economic development and maintaining social stability. In Jul. 2017, it was announced at the National Financial Work Conference to set up the Financial Stability and Development Committee under the State Council. This was an important decision for China to build a stable financial system which aimed to strengthen financial supervision and coordination, correct and improve drawbacks, enhance PBC's responsibilities for macro-prudential regulation and systematic risk prevention, put into practice the regulatory functions of financial regulation agencies, intensify oversight and accountability and ensure safe and stable development of finance. To catch up traditional international financial centers, Shanghai must actively promote the reform of economic and financial structure, establish perfect, stable and transparent financial system, drive legal construction to provide a just, fair and open legal environment for the finance industry and make efforts to improve urban development matching capacity and urban service level suited to the development of an international financial center.

3.5.3 Supporting the development of real economy

Real economy is the root of finance while finance is the blood vessel of real economy. The reports of the 19th National Congress of the Communist Party of China require to deepen institutional reform in the financial sector and make it better serve the real economy. As is stressed, finance should return to its original purpose of serving economic and social development. In the current and future periods, it is necessary to set the service for the real economy as the start point and foothold and comprehensively enhance the quality and efficiency of finance to serve the real economy. In the process of building an international financial center, Shanghai needs to provide more support to the development of real economy, allocate more financial resources to key fields and weak links of economic and social development, better meet diversified financial demands of the masses and the real economy, and regard the achievements of serving the real economy as an important index for measuring financial performance.

3.5.4 Perfecting the financial market system

With the economic development and deepening of financial market in recent years, financial opening-up of our country has made a series of substantial progress. The new open type economic system is progressively refined; foreign trade, foreign investment and foreign currency reserve remain stable forefront of the world; and RMB enjoys an increasingly higher international standing. As pointed out at the National Financial Work Conference 2017, we will expand financial opening-up, deepen the reform of RMB exchange rate formation mechanism, steadily promote

RMB internationalization and achieve capital account convertibility. Also as noted, China will not close its door to the world; we will only become more and more open. Financial market infrastructure is not only the basis for smoothening currency policy transmission mechanism, accelerating turnover of social funds and maintaining the stability of financial system, but the guarantee for financial center to improve its function in allocating financial resources. At present, the construction of Shanghai International Financial Center is at a critical transitional period from expanding the scale to focusing on quality and from gathering resources to improving functions. Therefore, the construction of financial market infrastructure appears particularly crucial. Shanghai will accelerate the construction of an international financial center suited to the international standing of RMB, effectively expand the breadth and depth of RMB product market, enrich RMB products and instruments, improve the market scale and influence of RMB products, and support the construction of global RMB benchmark price formation center, asset management center, payment and clearing center and risk management center.

Chapter IV

Building Shanghai into a High-quality International Financial Center in the New Era of Opening-up

President Xi Jinping's report to the 19th CPC National Congress states that by 2020 China will finish building a moderately prosperous society in all respects and achieve the first centenary goal; similarly, the *Shanghai's 13th Five-year Plan* adopted by the State Council stipulates that by 2020 Shanghai will be developed into an international financial center that is commensurate with China's economic strength and Renminbi's international status and rank among leading global financial centers.

What has happened proves that the opening-up is key to China's economic growth over the past 40 years and in the same vein, high-quality development of China's economy in the future can only be achieved with greater openness. At the Boao Forum for Asia Annual Conference 2018, President Xi Jinping delivered a keynote speech titled "Openness for Greater Prosperity, Innovation for a Better Future", making clear China's firm will and resolve to deepen reform and opening-up. In a new era of opening-up, Shanghai should grasp the historical opportunity and take the initiative towards the building of a high-quality international financial center with a host of innovative and result-oriented measures, so as to serve the new ground in comprehensive opening-up and create a new regime of open economy.

4.1 Easing the Market Access for Financial Sector

At the Bo'ao Forum for Asia Annual Conference 2018, President Xi Jinping solemnly announced a host of major measures to ease the market access for the financial sector and other industries. For services, financial services in particular, important announcement was made at the end of 2017 on measures to raise foreign equity caps in the banking, securities and insurance industries. It is important to ensure that these measures are materialized and at the same time make more moves toward further opening, including accelerating the opening-up of the insurance industry, easing restrictions on the establishment of foreign financial institutions in China and expanding their business scope, and opening up more areas of cooperation between Chinese and foreign financial markets.

4.1.1 Moving Shanghai towards an international financial center featuring greater openness, coverage and influence through "renewed commitment to reform and opening-up"

On April 13, the Standing Committee of the CPC Shanghai Municipal Committee held an enlarged meeting to convey and study the spirit of Xi's keynote speech at the Bo'ao Forum for Asia and his important speech on celebrating the 30th anniversary of the founding of Hainan Province and the Hainan Special Economic Zone, in a bid to uphold the banner of reform and opening-up, reaffirm its confidence and resolve to "renew the commitment to reform and opening-up", take the lead and add substance to the major initiative of reform and opening-up. Meanwhile, the municipal government held an executive meeting to draw up a pilot plan for easing the market access for the financial sector and urge the implementation of the timetable and roadmap for a host of projects in this regard. According to Li Qiang, the Secretary of CPC Shanghai Municipal Committee, from the perspective of agglomerating the driving capacities, high quality development is about staying committed to the direction of functional development, enhancing the city's core functions, and accelerating the building of an international center of economy, finance, trade, shipping and scientific and technological innovation ("five-center initiative"), so Shanghai needs to allocate global resources while driving the regional economic development; with the increasingly tighter restraints on land resources and environment and the soaring cost of business and production, Shanghai should align itself to the highest standard around the world, enhance the soft power of institutional environment and bring its business environment to new heights, so as to become more attractive, creative and competitive; moreover, Shanghai should follow the requirements of the Central Government to accelerate the building of an international center of economy, finance, trade, shipping and scientific and technological innovation, an excellent international city and a socialist modern international metropolis featuring global influence, so that it will be in a better position to take part in international cooperation and competition on behalf of the nation amid efforts to deepen reform and opening-up in various areas in the new era, and contribute more to enhancing China's institutional say in the global economic governance system. Ying Yong, the Mayor of Shanghai, stressed that Shanghai should sprint towards an international financial center between now and 2020. He added that Shanghai must move faster towards an international financial center featuring greater openness, driving capacity and influence with a forward-looking approach in line with the trend of profound transformation of global economy and finance, the bigger picture of efforts to deepen reform and opening-up across the board, and the country's strategic plan for Shanghai's development.

(1) It is necessary to continue with the priority of opening-up, implement a more proactive strategy of opening-up and accelerate the building of a new regime of open economy. Openness is the biggest strength of Shanghai. It is important to grasp the important opportunity brought by the Central Government's commitment to greater openness, take the initiative to launch pilot programs for opening up the service industry, and enhance the financial market's function to allocate global resources. In addition to advancing the building of a pilot free trade zone, it is necessary to move faster to link our system and mechanism with the international prevailing rules, work for high-level trade and investment liberalization and facilitation, and serve as a bridgehead for serving the Belt and Road Initiative and encouraging companies to "go global".

(2) It is necessary to promote the opening-up of the financial services in a broader scope, on a wider range of areas and at a higher level. A financial innovation system that is suited to a more open environment and can effectively guard against risks has been established by giving full play to the test field of Shanghai Pilot Free Trade Zone and steadily taking a series of financial reform measures, including building a free trade account system, facilitating cross-border investment, financing and remittance, and creating a market-oriented financial sector. It is necessary to continue with the in-depth linkage between the pilot free trade zone and the building of an international financial center, and serve the Renminbi internationalization process in a proactive manner while keeping risks under control. It is also essential to further implement the *Plan for Further Promoting the Pilot Project of Financial Opening-up and Innovation in China (Shanghai) Pilot Free Trade Zone and Accelerating the Building of Shanghai International Financial Center*, move faster to build an international financial

market system and a Renminbi global service system, properly advance the pilot program for capital account convertibility, and continue to deepen the financial opening-up efforts.

(3) It is necessary to accelerate the building of Shanghai International Financial Center featuring persistent innovation and greater vitality, and strive for more substance to this initiative. As Shanghai is on the way towards a scientific and technological innovation center with global influence, science and technology is closely linked with finance to further unleash the fusion effect of coordinated innovation. On one hand, encouraging the further integration of financing into the innovation chain and industrial chain diversifies the means of financial support and service, which contribute to the building of Shanghai into a scientific and technological innovation center. With the implementation of a host of financial support policies on investment and loan linkage, scientific and technological insurance, and scientific and technological innovation over the years, innovation and entrepreneurship initiatives have yielded fruitful outcomes. On the other hand, it is necessary to rely on scientific and technological progress to accelerate the innovation of financial services and products, so that new financial business models will become a growing driving force for the building of Shanghai International Financial Center.

(4) It is necessary to build Shanghai into a more inclusive international financial center that enjoys deepened cooperation and benefits all. Cooperation adds dimensions to the development of Shanghai as a financial center. The Central Government requests the Shanghai Pilot Free Trade Zone to serve as a bridgehead for promoting the Belt and Road Initiative and encouraging market entities to go global, which offers a broader stage for the building of Shanghai International Financial Center. In this process, Shanghai should move faster to enhance the investment and financing service functions of its financial market, be proactive to deepen

its cooperation with financial institutions in countries and regions along the Belt and Road, and step up strategic cooperation with overseas offshore RMB markets, with a view to building it as an important hub for the allocation of domestic and foreign financial resources. Shanghai should join hands with world-famous financial cities to support the Belt and Road Initiative and work for a financial cooperation network based on mutual benefit and win-win outcomes, so as to share the outcomes of the building of Shanghai International Financial Center with more regions and their people.

4.1.2 Building Shanghai into a high-quality international financial center is the core of Shanghai's "five-center initiative"

Finance is Shanghai's core function as a city, which means that the building of Shanghai as a financial center is key to its "five-center initiative". In order for Shanghai to foster strategic strengths for its development and enhance the visibility of its "four-brands initiative" (Shanghai Service, Shanghai Manufacturing, Shanghai Shopping and Shanghai Culture), it is essential to work for the high-quality development of its financial sector. While staying committed to building an international and market-oriented financial system based on the rule of law, it is necessary to work to add more substance to the building of Shanghai as a financial center. Under the principle that the financial sector should serve the entity economy, it is important to further the reform, opening-up and innovation-driven development of the financial sector, while warding off and mitigating major risks. The target is to finish building Shanghai into an international financial center that is substantially commensurate with China's economic strength and RMB's international status and make it a leading global financial center by 2020.

In the new era, it is necessary to have a full grasp of the change of our major social contradictions, be proactive to adapt to the basic characteristic and fundamental requirement of the transformation of China's economy from high-speed growth to high-quality development, work for the high-quality development of the financial sector, and provide high-quality financial services for the development of other fields. It is important to follow the national strategy, act in line with the set targets, and accelerate the building of Shanghai International Financial Center; focus on accelerating the building of an RMB product market by pursuing the building of a market system as the target; focus on building a cluster of the headquarters of functional financial institutions by adhering to the agglomeration of financial institutions as the priority; and with financial environment optimization as the focus, make greater efforts to foster a business environment where business entities enjoy the freedom of operation without violating rules and have their concerns attended to, and continue with the improvement of the talent policies. Finance is the bloodline for the entity economy, so it is necessary to give full play to Shanghai's financial strengths when it comes to consolidating and enhancing the level of entity economy, strengthen the linkage between the building of Shanghai as a financial center and the building of Shanghai as a pilot free trade zone and a scientific and technological innovation center, and enable the financial sector to better serve the Belt and Road Initiative as well as the building of the Yangtze River economic zone. In addition, it is essential to promote the innovative development of finance while ensuring financial security and guarding against risks.

In order to advance Shanghai's reform and opening-up across the board, continuously improve the openness of Shanghai's financial sector and promote the building of Shanghai International Financial Center in various fields, it is necessary to focus on the following three aspects.

(1) Continuously improve the financial development and business

environment, enhance the visibility of Shanghai's financial services, and work for the sound development of the financial sector. It is necessary to take the initiative to provide foreign financial institutions with detailed supporting services, and work for the early implementation of opening-up projects. It is also necessary to sustain an open, transparent and inclusive financial business environment, so as to develop Shanghai into a platform for the country's commitment to greater openness and a gathering place for major foreign financial institutions.

(2) Deepen the financial reform, and undertake more pilot programs to broaden market access. 2018 marks the 40th anniversary of China's reform and opening-up. In a new round of reform and opening-up, Shanghai will take the lead and responsibility to align the building of Shanghai International Financial Center with the financial opening-up and innovation of the pilot free trade zone, actively undertake state pilot programs on new financial products, business innovation and Fin Tech, work for the high-quality development of the financial sector, and better serve the entity economy. Meanwhile, it is important to prepare financial innovation for risk stress testing, and take concrete actions to hold the bottomline of risk prevention.

(3) Pursue development through opening-up, and make new progress in the building of Shanghai International Financial Center. It is necessary to accelerate the building of an international financial market system and the building of a global center for innovation, transaction, pricing and settlement of RMB products. It is also necessary to continuously enhance Shanghai's international influence as an international financial center and its ability to allocate global resources through opening-up, and accelerate the building of Shanghai into an international financial center that is commensurate with China's economic strength and RMB's international status, so as to provide new opportunities for and inject new impetus into

economic globalization.

4.1.3 Shanghai's measures to increase opening-up and encourage pilot programs to build an international financial center

It is a state strategy to build Shanghai International Financial Center. The city has been leading the country in the opening-up of the financial sector. In light of the opening-up measures for the financial sector announced by the People's Bank of China, Shanghai has come up with a list of measures to increase openness, seeking to undertake pilot programs in the following six areas.

First, Shanghai will increase the openness of its banking sector with a host of measures, including supporting foreign banks' efforts to simultaneously establish branches and subsidiaries in Shanghai, supporting commercial banks' efforts to set up financial assets investment companies and wealth management firms in Shanghai whose foreign shareholding ratio is not limited, and supporting foreign banks in conducting commissioned distribution and commissioned payment.

Second, Shanghai will increase the openness of its securities sector with such measures as supporting the establishment of foreign-controlled securities companies, funds companies and futures companies in Shanghai and allowing them to engage in brokerage and consultancy.

Third, Shanghai will increase the openness of its insurance sector with a series of measures, including removing the restrictions on the business scope for foreign insurance brokers in Shanghai, supporting foreign companies in operating as insurance brokers and accessors in Shanghai, and supporting the establishment of foreign-controlled life insurance firms.

Fourth, Shanghai will increase the openness of its financial market with such measures as supporting foreign investors in participating in Shanghai's securities market, supporting foreign innovative enterprises in issuing Chinese Depositary Receipts (CDR) in Shanghai, striving for the launch of the Shanghai-London Stock Connect initiative, and further expanding the scale of Panda Bonds.

Fifth, Shanghai will expand the function and use scope of FT accounts. An RMB global service system will be developed based on RMB internationalization. In this process, Shanghai will strive to extend FT accounts to pilot free trade zones in the Yangtze River delta region and the Yangtze River economic zone, and expand the investment and financing functions of FT accounts.

Sixth, Shanghai will ease the market access for bank card clearing houses and non-bank payment institutions, and remove the ban on foreign financial service companies providing credit rating services.

On April 27, 2018, the China Banking and Insurance Regulatory Commission made it clear that foreign insurance brokers can apply with the local insurance regulatory bureaus for business license change following the removal of restrictions on the business scope. The Shanghai Bureau of China Insurance Regulatory Commission reviewed and approved the application for the change in the business scope from Willis Insurance Brokers Co., Ltd., a controlled company of Willis Group, making it the first foreign insurance broker to obtain the approval on expanding its business scope. On April 28, Oney Bank and Bright Food Group inked an investment agreement to establish Shanghai Bright-Oney Consumer Finance Co., Ltd., which will be the first consumer finance company set up in China by European and American entities. On May 2, the China Banking and Insurance Regulatory Commission formally approved the establishment of ICBC-AXA Asset Management Company proposed by ICBC-AXA LIFE, which is the first joint-venture insurance asset management company approved since China proposed to speed up the opening process of the insurance industry. On May 8, Nomura Holdings Inc. submitted an application with China Securities Regulatory Commission (CSRC) to set up a foreign investment securities company in which Nomura Holdings plans to hold 51% of the shares. JPMorgan Chase also submitted an application with CSRC to establish a foreign securities broker in Shanghai. On May 9, the headquarters of Allianz SE decided to set up a wholly-owned Allianz (China) Insurance Group Company in Shanghai.

4.1.4 The openness of financial sector should match with the capacity of financial supervision

A financial center is a funds pooling center and transaction center, and it may also become a risk center. An international financial center, if regulated well, will become an important hub for international finance; however, without necessary regulation, it may become a worst-hit area. As such, it is important to emphasize risk prevention and control. Han Zheng, a Member of the Standing Committee of the Political Bureau and the Vice Premier of the State Council, pointed out that Shanghai free trade zone should further promote the building of Shanghai International Financial Center, and that relevant measures should be further deepened and improved. One important thing is that Shanghai should carry out financial reform and innovation while keeping risks under control, which is the fundamental adherence.

Governor Yi Gang of the People's Bank of China said at the China Development Forum on March 25, 2018 that three rules should be followed to increase the opening-up of the financial sector: first, as a competitive service sector, the financial sector should follow the principles of pre-establishment national treatment and negative list; second, the opening-up of the financial sector and the reform of the exchange rate formation mechanism and the capital account process should support and reinforce each other; third, equal importance should be attached to the openness of the financial sector and the prevention of financial risks. The openness of the financial sector should match with the capacity of financial supervision.

Efforts to increase the opening-up of the financial sector should be adapted to the improvement of financial regulation and financial market system, and they should be coordinated with the opening-up of relevant financial areas. The opening-up of the financial system will inevitably destabilize the financial market. Therefore, a well-developed macro prudential regulation framework that is commensurate with the opening-up of the financial system should be in place to effectively ward off and mitigate various risks that accompany the process of financial opening-up, the cross-border capital flow risks in particular. In this process, it is necessary to substantiate the policy toolkit for macro prudential management of cross-border capital flows, including the management tools targeted at reducing the large fluctuations of cross-border capital (such as loan loss provision) and the macro prudential management policies focusing on banks and short-term capital flows to make counter-cyclic adjustment to short-term fluctuations of the foreign exchange market, so as to maintain the security of the financial system and the balance of international payments.

4.2 Explore the Building of Free Trade Port

China (Shanghai) Pilot Free Trade Zone (hereinafter referred to as "Shanghai Pilot Free Trade Zone") represents a major initiative to deepen reform and opening-up proposed by the Central Party Committee and State Council under new circumstances. On March 30, 2017, the State Council issued the *Plan for Comprehensively Deepening the Reform and Opening up of China (Shanghai) Pilot Free Trade Zone*, which sets the targets for the reform and opening-up of Shanghai Pilot Free Trade Zone between now and 2020, ushering in a new stage for the building of Shanghai Pilot Free Trade Zone.

4.2.1 Progress has been made in the financial system innovation targeted at capital account convertibility and financial opening-up

First, progress has been made in the financial opening-up and innovation with free trade accounts (FT accounts) as its core. The FT account system is the fundamental system and the the most prominent highlight for the financial opening-up and innovation of Shanghai Pilot Free Trade Zone. This system can not only provide cross-border domestic and foreign currency settlement service under current account and direct investment, but also conduct such business as overseas financing, cross-border certificate of deposit and interest rate swap. Since its establishment and operation, the FT account system has realized the "primary prudential regulation and secondary limited penetration" of cross-border capital flows through the separate accounting system and FT accounts, laying an important foundation for promoting RMB capital account convertibility. By the end of December, 2017, a total of 56 financial institutions in Shanghai Pilot Free Trade Zone had passed the acceptance of separate accounting system; 70,200 FT accounts had been established; the financing amount had totaled CNY 1.1 trillion; and the account fund balance had been CNY 217.6 billion.

Second, progress has been made in the reform of the foreign exchange management system, and the cross-border use of RMB has been expanded gradually. As for the foreign exchange fund pool and the removal of the restrictions on credit and debt management, foreign trade and investment have been greatly facilitated by improving the central operation and management of foreign exchange funds for international companies and the management of foreign exchange settlement and sales, and simplifying the procedure of foreign exchange receipt and payment under current account. Shanghai is the first to establish a macro prudential overseas financing system featuring domestic and foreign currency integration, with steady progress in such new businesses as overseas borrowing in RMB and cross-border two-way RMB capital pool and in rapid development of cross-border RMB businesses.

Third, the openness of the financial market and services has been improved. Supported by the financial system innovation strengths of the pilot free trade zone, Shanghai continues expanding the opening-up scope of its financial services sector and allowing the financial market to better allocate resources at home and abroad. On one hand, steady progress has been made in the building of such international financial transaction platforms as the Shanghai-Hong Kong Stock Connect, the International Business of Shanghai Gold Exchange and Shanghai International Energy Exchange, and the pricing and trading mechanism has been improved. On the other hand, the financial services sector has advanced its opening-up both internally and externally, as evidenced by the support of China Banking Regulatory Commission for Chinese and foreign banking financial institutions operating in the pilot free trade zone and the efforts of China Securities Regulatory Commission and China Insurance Regulatory Commission to promote the clustered development of securities, futures and insurance institutions in the pilot free trade zone.

Fourth, the capacities of financial regulation and risk prevention and control have been improved. Shanghai has further improved the measures for macro prudential management of the financial sector and the mechanism of risk prevention among financial institutions, and each financial opening-up and innovation measure is accompanied by a corresponding financial regulation system. For example, the Shanghai

Head Office of the People's Bank of China, together with relevant departments, has set up an inter-department mechanism of cross-border capital monitoring and analysis as well as emergency coordination to step up the monitoring and risk prevention of cross-border capital flows; the Shanghai Office of China Banking Regulatory Commission has set up a consumer rights and interests protection system covering sales, complaint and investigation; Shanghai Municipal Financial Service Office, together with relevant departments, has introduced the detailed rules for the implementation of comprehensive financial supervision, so as to move faster towards a comprehensive regulatory model for information interconnection and sharing.

4.2.2 More efforts are needed to advance the financial opening-up and innovation of Shanghai Pilot Free Trade Zone

Financial opening-up and innovation are the priorities of the opening-up for the pilot free trade zone. Despite remarkable progress in the building of Shanghai Pilot Free Trade Zone, much work is still required to realize capital account convertibility and an open financial services sector. Because the detailed rules or innovation cases have yet to be specified regarding some items in the *Plan for Further Promoting the Pilot Project of Financial Opening-up and Innovation in China (Shanghai) Pilot Free Trade Zone and Accelerating the Building of Shanghai International Financial Center*, relevant work is progressing slowly; although Shanghai has decided to extend FT account business across the city, all the companies with a FT account are only operating in the pilot free trade zone; the FT account is mainly used in the current account, and has strict restrictions on capital and financial account transactions, so some financial institutions do not respond positively to the FT account; although the regional headquarters of international companies in the pilot free trade zone have great demands for facilitating the foreign exchange receipt and payment of transit trade and offshore trade, the pilot free trade zone is tightening up its foreign exchange management policy on new business models of trade.

In his report at the 19th CPC National Congress, President Xi Jinping said, "We must actively participate in and promote economic globalization, develop an open economy of higher standards, and continue to increase China's economic power and composite strength." He also stated, "It is necessary to make new ground in pursuing opening-up on all fronts. We will adopt policies to promote high-standard liberalization and facilitation of trade and investment; we will implement the system of pre-establishment national treatment plus a negative list across the board, significantly ease market access, further open the services sector, and protect the legitimate rights and interests of foreign investors. We will grant more powers to pilot free trade zones to conduct reform, and explore the opening of free trade ports." In his keynote speech at the Opening Ceremony of the Bo'ao Forum for Asia Annual Conference 2018, President Xi said that the Chinese people will continue increasing openness and expanding cooperation, pay equal attention to "bringing in" and "going global", break new ground in opening China further through links running eastward and westward, across land and over sea, adopt policies to promote high-standard liberalization and facilitation of trade and investment, and explore the opening of free trade ports with Chinese characteristics.

At present, Shanghai Pilot Free Trade Zone is in a key period for further promotion. The Central Government requested Shanghai Pilot Free Trade Zone to make audacious experiments and adventures and independently make changes towards the most open free trade zone featuring convenient investment and trade, free currency exchange, efficient and convenient regulation as well as standardized legal environment. President Xi made it clear that institutional innovation represents the core task of the building of a pilot free trade zone, and that we should learn from the highest-standard and highest-level free trade zones across the world, improve basic system, overcome bottlenecks, address difficulties, activate all fronts, take the lead to foster a law-based, international and convenient business environment, and accelerate the building of a fair, unified and efficient market environment. These requirements chart the course for the building of Shanghai Pilot Free Trade Zone.

4.2.3 Strengthening the linkage between the financial reform of Shanghai Pilot Free Trade Zone and the building of Shanghai International Financial Center

Shanghai Pilot Free Trade Zone is closely linked with the building of Shanghai International Financial Center. To become a center for trading, pricing, clearing, settlement and product innovation of RMB financial assets, Shanghai should give full play to the institutional strength of Shanghai Pilot Free Trade Zone, move forward the opening of the financial market and financial product innovation, and accelerate capital account convertibility and RMB internationalization relying on the FT account system. To increase its agglomeration capacity as an international financial center, Shanghai should give full play to' the function of Shanghai Pilot Free Trade Zone in financial institution innovation, so as to provide strong support for the building of Shanghai International Financial Center.

First, continue increasing the openness of financial services sector and financial market. Shanghai will increase the two-way openness of its financial market, support China Foreign Exchange Trade Center, Shanghai Stock Exchange and Shanghai Gold Exchange in establishing international financial transaction platforms in Shanghai's financial market, and provide more channels for foreign investors, especially institutional investors of long-term funds, to participate in the domestic financial market, and encourage domestic enterprises and individuals to "go global".

Second, expand financial service functions. Shanghai will move faster to explore an institutional environment that supports the development of offshore trade and service trade, establish a domestic and foreign account management system suitable for Shanghai Pilot Free Trade Zone, and promote the facilitation of cross-border trade, investment, financing and settlement. Shanghai will also explore a comprehensive commodity trade platform to integrate the transaction functions of international and domestic markets, increase the accessibility of commodity transactions and capital transactions, and support innovative cross-border RMB businesses in the field of commodities, including RMB pricing and settlement as well as cross-border two-way RMB capital pool.

Third, explore RMB internationalization. Shanghai will improve the institutional rules and operation schemes to broaden the channels of cross-border investment and financing in RMB, promote the RMB Cross-border Payment System (CIPS), establish and improve the cross-border two-way flow mechanism for RMB capital, advance the cross-border use of RMB, improve the system for international settlement in RMB, and increase the proportion of RMB in the settlement transaction of financial products.

Fourth, further expand FT account functions. Shanghai will assist the People's Bank of China and other relevant departments in further expanding and improving FT account functions, start businesses of domestic and foreign current integration under FT accounts at an early date, and encourage and support banking, securities and insurance financial institutions' efforts to conduct financial innovation business with

FT accounts. Shanghai will explore the pilot project of convertibility within limits and implement the pilot project of foreign investment by qualified domestic individual investors in Shanghai Pilot Free Trade Zone. Shanghai will also further optimize and simplify the procedure of funds transfer under FT accounts, so as to make it more accessible.

Fifth, study and development a negative list of the financial services sector. The opening of China's financial market is restricted by the domestic system, laws and market rules. Shanghai Pilot Free Trade Zone should align itself with the high-standard international business and trade rules, move faster to improve the negative list system of market access for the financial sector, open the financial services sector wider to qualified private investors and foreign institutions, and carry out mixed operation in the financial sector while guarding off risks to build a financial factor market.

4.2.4 Further improving the risk control system that is suited to an open economy

Financial security is an important component of national security, and it represents the important foundation for the steady and sound development of the economy. In the process of deepening the financial reform of Shanghai Pilot Free Trade Zone, attention should be paid to ward off financial risks, build a financial regulation mechanism that is suited to the linkage between the development of Shanghai Pilot Free Trade Zone and the building of Shanghai International Financial Center, strengthen protection against financial risks, and create a safe and stable environment for financial development. This is of great importance to the building of Shanghai International Financial Center.

First, step up financial coordinated regulation and explore functional regulation in Shanghai Pilot Free Trade Zone. Shanghai will give further play to the role of a financial coordination mechanism consisting of national financial management authorities' branches in Shanghai and relevant local departments, step up cross-department, cross-industry and cross-market financial regulation and information sharing, and take the lead to explore a new mechanism of financial regulation coordination between the Central Government and the local government.

Second, encourage greater involvement of national financial departments in market supervision. Shanghai will encourage national financial departments to set up subsidiary head offices in Shanghai, delegate the functions of regulating the market and facilitating product innovation to financial regulators in Shanghai and its financial market, and support national financial management departments in authorizing their regulatory institutions in Shanghai to extend the pilot projects of financial reform beyond Shanghai Pilot Free Trade Zone and across the city.

Third, change the way in which financial innovation is regulated. Shanghai will reduce items requiring administrative approval, simplify pre-access items, support financial institutions' independent innovation efforts, and step up in-operation and post-operation analysis and evaluation. Shanghai will also encourage financial institutions to independently develop new products that are yet to be restricted by current laws and regulations, and make independent decisions and conduct business on the basis of thorough independent assessment of risks.

Fourth, step up financial risk prevention. In light of the progress of the financial opening-up and innovation of Shanghai Pilot Free Trade Zone and the building of Shanghai International Financial Center, Shanghai will make active efforts to improve the mechanism for monitoring and analyzing cross-border capital flows, and step up the working mechanism on anti-money laundering, anti-terrorist financing and anti-tax evasion. In light of the characteristic of cross-industry, cross-market and cross-border development of financial institutions, Shanghai will adhere to the principle of financial prudential exception, take the initiative of financial opening-up, and establish and improve the system for early warning, prevention and mitigation of systematic risks.

Fifth, improve the financial infrastructure system. Shanghai will advance the systems regarding the central counterparties and trade information report databases in the financial market, and improve the system for registration, custody, transaction, clearing and settlement of financial products. Shanghai will also coordinate the development of payment, clearing and settlement systems, further step up the efficient processing and transfer of data among the issuing system, transaction system, clearing system, custody and settlement system, internal system of market entities and monitoring system of the regulator, enhance the functions of relevant basic technology systems, and improve market transparency and operational efficiency.

Sixth, improve the financial credit system. Shanghai will introduce high-level credit rating institutions, encourage the diversified development of credit reporting agencies, actively use new technology to develop new business models of credit, and encourage the development of credit products that meet market demands. Shanghai will also step up the protection of financial consumers' rights and interests, establish and improve the working mechanism on protecting the rights and interests of financial consumers, explore a diversity of models to resolve financial consumption disputes, and set up a mechanism to foster synergy between departments to incorporate emerging financial areas into consumer protection.

4.3 Building Shanghai into a Global Scientific and Technological Innovation Center

Building a scientific and technological innovation center with global influence is the important foundation for Shanghai to implement the innovation-driven development strategy. President Xi Jinping pointed out that Shanghai should focus on stepping up the systematic integration of measures to deepen reform and opening-up across the board, and on moving faster towards a scientific and technological innovation center with global influence. The Central Government set the target of developing Shanghai into a scientific and technological innovation center with global influence, which requires the financial sector to provide more support for scientific and technological innovation. The process of building Shanghai as a scientific and technological innovation center will contribute to the business of financial market and financial institutions and promote the development of the capital market.

To provide capital support and financial innovation services for the building of Shanghai as a global scientific and technological innovation center, Shanghai needs to step up the linkage between the building of Shanghai International Financial Center, the development of Shanghai free trade zone and the building of Shanghai as a scientific and technological center with global influence. In turn, the process of building Shanghai as a scientific and technological innovation center will attract more financial institutions to Shanghai International Financial Center, contribute to financial innovations such as investment and loan linkage as well as financing guarantee, and promote the development of Fin Tech and multi-level capital market.

4.3.1 Improving ecological environment for the building of Shanghai into a scientific and technological innovation center of financial services

In 2017, Shanghai issued the *Action Plan* (2017 - 2020) *of Shanghai's Banking Industry to Support the Building of Shanghai Scientific and Technological Innovation Center*, which specifies the development strategy, key tasks and planning targets that the banking industry will follow to support the building of Shanghai as a scientific and technological innovation center, and makes it clear that "by the end of 2020, the loan balance of scientific and technological enterprises within Shanghai's jurisdiction will reach around CNY 270 billion, up by 80% from the end of 2016; and the banking industry will fully support the building of Shanghai as a scientific and technological innovation center with global influence."

Shanghai's capital market has also provided strong support for scientific and technological innovation. The pilot project of "entrepreneurship and innovation bond" was launched to support the setting of share transfer terms for privately issued innovation and entrepreneurship bonds; preferential tax policies were introduced for venture investment funds and angel investors; differential reduction policy was introduced to support the venture investment fund shareholders of listed companies, and mobilize the enthusiasm of venture investment funds for long-term investment and value investment through reverse link; CDR was introduced, and a host of rules and innovative products were launched to encourage the return of overseas listed "unicorns". All these have created a capital market regulation environment that is more inclusive to new economy, which will contribute to accelerating the efficiency conversion of scientific and technological innovation enterprises. In 2017, Shanghai added 56 listed companies, among which 44 are scientific and technological innovation enterprises, accounting for nearly 80%; listed companies engaged in scientific and technological innovation raised nearly CNY 100 billion through IPO or refinancing to support independent innovation, industrial upgrade and technological progress; 9 scientific and technological innovation enterprises raised over CNY 11.7 billion by issuing corporate bonds; 15 scientific and technological innovation enterprises used the capital market to conduct mergers and acquisitions worth of CNY 46.86 billion; the New Third

Board added 58 scientific and technological innovation enterprises from Shanghai, which raised CNY 3.85 billion; and enterprises listed on the scientific and technological innovation board of Shanghai Equity Exchange totaled 171, among which 110 realized nearly CNY 1.1 billion of equity financing and 139 realized nearly CNY 900 million of debt financing through bank credit loan, equity pledge loan and technology performance loan. By the end of 2017, ongoing projects of private equity investment fund and venture investment fund managed by registered private equity fund managers in Shanghai totaled nearly 10,800, of which half are at the seed stage or start stage, with an investment principal of over CNY 720 billion. This solved the problem of "last mile" for many scientific and technological innovation enterprises.

4.3.2 Supporting the building of Shanghai into a scientific and technological innovation center through expanding financial opening-up and financial reform innovation

First, actively advance investment and loan linkage. In April 2016, China Banking Regulatory Commission and other relevant ministries issued the Guiding Opinions on Supporting Banking Financing Institutions in Enhancing Their Efforts in Innovation and Launching the Pilot Program of Linking Investments and Loans for Enterprises Engaging in Scientific Innovation, identifying the Zhangjiang National Innovation Demonstration Zone as one of the first batch of regions to launch the pilot project of investment and loan linkage and including 3 banks within its jurisdiction in the first batch of banks to launch the pilot project of investment and loan linkage. By the end of 2017, the number of outstanding loan accounts under investment and loan linkage was 315, an increase of 132 accounts or 72.12% from the end of 2016; the loan balanced reached CNY 6.090 billion, an increase of CNY 3.477 billion or 133.06% from the end of

2016. Since 2016, banking financial institutions have provide 391 scientific and technological innovation enterprises with investment and loan linkage services, granting CNY 13.922 billion of loans in total.

Second, a risk compensation mechanism that supports scientific and technological innovation through finance has been established. Shanghai established the Policy Financing Guarantee Fund for Micro, Small and Medium-sized Enterprises in Shanghai, which provides guarantee for the credit of micro, small and medium-sized enterprises in Shanghai, those engaging in science and technology in particular, and supports innovative enterprises and little giant enterprises certified by the national innovation fund, Shanghai municipal innovation fund and Shanghai Science and Technology Committee. By the end of 2017, 38 banks have established partnerships with the guarantee fund; and the fund granted CNY 5.641 billion of guaranteed loans, 3.86 times that in 2016. Shanghai formulated the Measures on Credit Risk Compensation for Scientific and Technological Micro-, Small-and Medium-Sized Enterprises in Shanghai, which stipulates that qualified scientific and technological micro-, small- and medium-sized enterprises are entitled to the risk loss compensation of the special financial fund of credit risk compensation for net loss of non-performing loans arising from granting of loans which exceeds a specified ratio. By the end of 2017, 36 commercial banks within Shanghai's jurisdiction have qualified for the pilot project of credit risk compensation; certified loan products under the pilot project of credit risk compensation totaled 154; compensation to pilot banks totaled CNY 85.98 million; and credit investment in scientific and technological micro, small and medium-sized enterprises has been strengthened. Shanghai also advanced the Innovation and Entrepreneurship Credit Enhancement Fund for Micro-and Small-sized Enterprises, encouraged financial institutions to finance scientific and technological enterprises, and promoted targeted use of financial resources in scientific and technological innovation.

Third, a life cycle financial support system has been established in light of the growth stage of enterprises. The strength of financial mixed operation enables commercial banks in Shanghai to provide all-round services including loans, investment, insurance and funds. For example, Shanghai Branch of the Bank of China has launched a service model of One-stop Investment and Loan Linkage, which links various direct investment institutions of Bank of China Group to realize multi-channel and multi-dimension investment service function, providing enterprises with the services of "credit factory, investment and loan linkage, and cross-border cooperation"; Shanghai Branch of China Construction Bank introduced a comprehensive service program of scientific innovation to design a package of comprehensive financial service plans suited to scientific and technological small-and medium-sized enterprises, practically improving the financing environment for scientific and technological small-and medium-sized enterprises. The Bank of Shanghai launched the Financing Plan for the Leaping Development of Enterprises Engaging in Scientific Innovation, which moves forward financial services based on the growth circle of scientific innovation enterprises and provides them with credit support at the beginning. The patient pledge loan business addresses the difficulties in financing for scientific and technological start-ups which lack guarantee, and plays a positive role in promoting the transformation of their scientific and technological achievements.

Fourth, Shanghai has provided guaranteed services to advance the development of scientific and technological enterprises. For example, Shanghai's insurance industry actively promoted the implementation of the science and technology insurance support policy, and formulated a special insurance plan associated with the first unit (set) of insurance, scientific and technological micro, small and medium-sized enterprises and core technical personnel. Shanghai has given full play to the fiscal subsidy mechanism, granting around CNY 30 million of science and technology insurance subsidies; the information sharing mechanism has been in full play, with Shanghai municipal science and technology financial information service platform sharing the financial credit data of 26,000 scientific and technological enterprises, improving the risk control level for science and technology insurance; Shanghai has launched such product series with fiscal supports as technology performance loan, micro-credit connect, finance lease liability insurance, biomedicine insurance and patent insurance to form a full-fledged insurance and guarantee system for science and technology. By the end of 2017, the technology performance loan has granted a total of 1,896 loans, which are valued at CNY 6.494 billion, to support 2, 242 scientific and technological enterprises; the guarantee amount of the first unit (set) of insurance exceeded CNY 10 billion; and the patent insurance has provided over CNY 35 million of risk guarantee for over 1,400 patent applications.

Fifth, Shanghai has stepped its cooperation with scientific and technological parks and venture capital institutions, which enjoy strong capabilities of operation and management as well as information strength, to cultivate and empower scientific and technological enterprises. For example, Shanghai Branch of the Industrial and Commercial Bank of China launched "Kejinhui", which follows the direction of accelerating the building of Shanghai as a Fin Tech functional zone to promote the rapid development of scientific and technological enterprises in the zone, advance the transformation of their scientific and technological achievements, and contribute to the economic development of scientific and technological micro, small, and medium-sized enterprises and the industry transformation and upgrading; Shanghai Branch of the Bank of Communications launched the "Investment and Loan Linkage for Scientific

Innovation Enterprises", which finance the capital demands of enterprises directly invested by its subsidiaries, guidance funds and shared funds arising from business turnover.

Sixth, contribute to the building of Shanghai as a scientific and technological innovation center by increasing the openness of its financial sector. Shanghai has actively encouraged foreign banks to participate in supporting scientific and technological innovation. By the end of 2017, the number of scientific and technological enterprises taking loans from foreign banks within Shanghai's jurisdiction was 477, an increase of 171 or 55.9% from the beginning of that year; the loan balance reached CNY 15.2 billion, an increase of CNY 6.08 billion or 66.6% from the beginning of that year.

4.4 Advancing the Belt and Road Initiative

4.4.1 Shanghai International Financial Center represents a financial bridgehead in advancing the Belt and Road Initiative

Its extensive financial connections with node cities in the global finance network system enables Shanghai International Financial Center to leverage its capability of global capital allocation to meet the huge capital demands of the Belt and Road Initiative. Through its market experience and innovation momentum, Shanghai is actively promoting the financial reform and innovation of the free trade zone, striving towards an investment and financing center and global RMB financial service center under the Belt and Road Initiative. By the end of 2017, the Cross-border Interbank Payment System (CIPS) has attracted 508 indirect participants from countries and regions along the Belt and Road, covering 41 countries and regions; cross-border receipts and payments with countries and regions along the Belt and Road through FT accounts totaled CNY 288.6 billion.

Shanghai Stock Exchange (SSE) worked with Kazakhstan to set up the Astana International Exchange, and a consortium established by SSE, China Financial Futures Exchange (CFFEX) and Shenzhen Stock Exchange (SZSE) became a strategic investor for the Pakistan Stock Exchange. What's more, an increasing number of enterprises from countries along the Belt and Road issued Panda bonds in Shanghai. The Dubai Gold & Commodities Exchange (DGCX) listed Shanghai Gold Futures Contract. Moreover, as Shanghai continues to step up its financial ties with countries and regions along the Belt and Road, relevant financial institutions have expressed strong will to set up their branch offices in Shanghai. By the end of the first quarter of 2018,5 legal person banks, 14 subsidiary banks and 9 representative offices from 15 countries along the Belt and Road, including Thailand, Malaysia, UAE and Kuwait are operating in Shanghai.

The *Action Plan on Building Shanghai as a Bridgehead in Serving the Belt and Road Initiative* stated that "we should build Shanghai into an investment and financing center and global RMB financial service center under the Belt and Road Initiative". Meanwhile, Shanghai is also on its way towards an important hub of optimized allocation of global financial factors, and represents a center of optimized allocation of key financial resources.

1) Financing center

Shanghai is home to licensed financial institutions and a host of systematic institutions and functional institutions such as Shanghai Head Office of the People's Bank of China, SSE, Shanghai Futures Exchange (SHFE), CFFEX and China UnionPay. This builds Shanghai into an internet financial center, providing project financing and entrepreneurial finance for the Belt and Road Initiative and promoting the integrated development of virtual economy and entity economy. As an International

Financial Center, Shanghai can diversify the means of financing supply. While giving full play to the role of Asian Infrastructure Investment Bank (AIIB), New Development Bank and Silk Road Fund in terms of supplying long-term funds, Shanghai has made great efforts to expand diversified financing channels, including private finance, insurance and fund sectors, international financing cooperation, domestic bank credit and bond direct financing market.

2) Investment center

Shanghai serves as a bridgehead in terms of encouraging Chinese business entities to go global and engage in overseas investment and development. From 2013 to 2017, Shanghai's direct foreign investment exceeded USD 67 billion, ranking the first in the country, with an obvious optimized structure. In this process, international companies based in Shanghai have emerged. In January 2018, a total of 78 direct foreign investment projects were filed with Shanghai; Chinese investment reached USD 1.017 billion, a year-on year increase of 1,044.1%. Shanghai is working to attract professional institutions to establish functional headquarters or regional headquarters, and build professional platforms and smart data platforms for project docking, so as to increase the implementation rate of projects under the Belt and Road Initiative. Shanghai has encouraged its financial sector to set up overseas institutions, with a view to breaking the bottleneck of overseas financial service. With a professional service capability to support direct foreign investment, Shanghai integrates such functions as consulting, overseas investment filing, investment project recommendation, investment destination introduction, industrial analysis and professional service for overseas investment, and can provide consulting services that meet the demands of corporate investors. It is working to attract law firms, accounting firms, banks, insurers and investment promotion institutions to provide service support for enterprises going global.

3) RMB financial service center

In the process of building the Belt and Road, Shanghai should step up the convertibility of RMB to other foreign currencies, strengthen the means of capital backflow, encourage clearing and settlement in RMB and innovate payment channels, to provide means for diversified investment of RMB in China. As an International Financial Center, Shanghai will develop RMB financial service products for industrial parks in the economic corridors along the Belt and Road, so as to increase the use of RMB. In the process of advancing the Belt and Road Initiative, Shanghai will make efforts to realize financial connectivity, facilitating the transition of the international development model for RMB from output under trade account to output under capital account. Shanghai will give full play to the role of financial institutions and international development institutions as financial intermediaries, so as to encourage enterprises going global to promote the use of RMB. At the same time, Shanghai will focus on linking RMB with entity economy, and drive RMB on its way towards the core of the allocation, production, sales, pricing and trading of global resources, so as to consolidate RMB's role as the basis for China's foreign trade and even international trade pricing and settlement currency. Shanghai will also explore the application of financial derivatives transaction to reduce the cost of capital and avoid the risks of interest and exchange rates, and capitalize on the cross-border linkage between domestic banks and overseas financial institutions to reduce the cost of source of foreign currency funds for domestic banks and support RMB going global.

4) Financial innovation center

The financial market's support for the Belt and Road Initiative will ultimately be realized by financial products. The circular of the National

Financial Work Conference 2017 mentioned that "relevant institutional design should be handled properly to promote financial innovation under the Belt and Road Initiative". The financial market system made up of the inter-bank market, foreign exchange market, SSE, CFFEX, SHFE, SGE and Shanghai Clearing House is Shanghai's advantage over other cities, and represents the precious resources that Shanghai can fully utilize when serving as the bridgehead for the Belt and Road Initiative. Since the Belt and Road Initiative was put forward, the financial market system has supported the Belt and Road Initiative through multiple modes, including exchange and training, share acquisition and new product development. Shanghai can fully utilize its financial market, or launch a new financial market and new financial products to support the flow of currencies, securities, futures and other financial products along the Belt and Road, so as to create an optimized allocation mechanism featuring high efficiency and low cost. To build Shanghai into an allocation center for financial resources under the Belt and Road Initiative, efforts should be made to form a system as early as possible, develop innovative products, build platforms and step up coordinated supervision.

4. 4. 2 Shanghai serving the Belt and Road Initiative as an international financial center: progress and prospect

General Secretary Xi Jinping called on Shanghai Pilot Free Trade Zone to become a bridgehead to promote the Belt and Road Initiative and encourage market entities going global. As an international financial center, Shanghai must make great efforts to support and serve the Belt and Road Initiative, and become the bridgehead to advance the initiative in terms of financial services. The Municipal Government of Shanghai has formulated and released the *Action Plan on Shanghai's Efforts to Serve as the Bridgehead in Serving the Belt and Road Initiative*, which calls on the city to actively response to the financial service demands of the initiative, innovate products and services, strengthen financial support for the initiative and enterprises going global, and provide them with omnidirectional cross-border financial services.

1) Remarkable progress has been made in the building of a cross-border currency payment and clearing system

First, the Global Association of Central Counterparties (CCP12) released the *CCP12 Template on Public Quantitative Disclosure* in Shanghai. Second, Phase II of CIPS has been accelerated, with greater participation of countries and regions along the Belt and Road. By March 2018, CIPS has 31 direct participants and 695 indirect participants (including 521 institutions from Asia, 88 institutions from Europe, 25 institutions from North America, 17 institutions from Oceania, 16 institutions from South America and 28 institutions from Africa). On the national level, CIPS' indirect participants comprise 161 financial institutions from 37 countries and regions along the Belt and Road (excluding Hong Kong and Macau SARs and Taiwan region), and its actual business has covered 731 legal person financial institutions from 51 countries and regions along the Belt and Road (excluding Hong Kong and Macau SARs and Taiwan region).

2) Major breakthroughs have been made in bond market financing under the Belt and Road Initiative

First, ChinaBond Pricing Center Co., Ltd. settled in Shanghai in July 2017. China Central Depository & Clearing Co., Ltd. (CCDC) opened its Shanghai headquarters, which integrates the five functional platforms, i. e. cross-border bond issurance center, cross-border settlement center, CCDC Collateral Management Service Center, ChinaBond Pricing Center and Shanghai Data Service Center, to further improve Shanghai's financial market system and serve the global RMB bond market. Second, the Bond

Connect was officially launched to increase the openness of China's bond market. In July 2017, the connectivity cooperation between mainland and Hong Kong bond markets (hereinafter referred as the Bond Connect) was officially put into trial operation. By the end of November 2017, 65 overseas institutional investors related to central banks and 291 overseas commercial institutional investors have entered the inter-bank bond market, and 161 overseas institutional investors have entered the inter-bank bond market by investing in the Bond Connect. Third, in March 2017, United Company RUSAL Plc (UC RUSAL) completed the issurance of the 2017 phase I corporate bonds with an issuing scale of CNY 1 billion at SSE, and was listed for transfer. This the first case of Panda Bonds issued by an enterprise from a country along the Belt and Road. In 2017, entities, including enterprises, banks and sovereign states, issued Panda Bonds on stock exchanges and inter-bank bond markets to contribute to the Belt and Road Initiative. Fourth, SSE issued the *Notice on Launching the Pilot Program of Bonds for the Belt and Road Initiative* to serve the government bonds issued on SSE by government institutions from countries (regions) along the Belt and Road; corporate bonds issued on SSE by enterprises and financial institutions from countries (regions) along the Belt and Road and corporate bonds issued on SSE by domestic and overseas enterprises for the purpose of raising money for the Belt and Road Initiative open a channel of direct financing through bonds for countries and regions, enterprises and projects under Belt and Road Initiative.

3) Synergy between financial innovation in free trade zone and the Belt and Road Initiative opens up a space for development

First, Shanghai issued the country's first guidelines on the negative list for opening the financial service industry in the pilot free trade zone to foreign investment, further broadening the entity scope of FT account. According to the *Guidelines on the Negative List for Opening the Financial*

Service Industry in China (*Shanghai*) *Pilot Free Trade Zone to Foreign Investment* (2017 *Edition*), the opening of the financial industry is more transparent and operable; the entity scope and functions of FT account are constantly expanded; the entity qualification of the account has been extended to enterprises with actual demands across the city, including entity enterprises serving the Belt and Road Initiative and going global, which have demands on international trade settlement and financing.

4) Exploring linkage between the Belt and Road Initiative and the building of Shanghai International Financial Center with a focus on stock exchange

First, in May 2017, a consortium established by CFFEC, SSE, SZSE, Pak-China Investment Company Limited and Habib Bank Limited successfully acquired 40% stock of the Pakistan Stock Exchange (PSX), making it the first case of Chinese capital market serving the Belt and Road Initiative. Pak-China Joint Investment Company Limited is the first joint investment company established by China in another developing country and the first overseas financial joint venture established by China Development Bank (CDB). As a joint venture built with USD 100 million from CDB and USD 100 million from the Ministry of Finance of Pakistan, it is aimed to deepen China-Pakistan cooperation in business, trade and finance. Second, in April 2018, Abu Dhabi Global Market (ADGM), the international financial centre of Abu Dhabi, UAE (ADGM) and Shanghai Stock Exchange (SSE), China's largest securities exchange, have entered into a Memorandum of Understanding (MOU) to co-operate on the establishment of a "Belt and Road" Exchange in ADGM. This co-operation harnesses Abu Dhabi's strategic position along the Silk Road Economic Belt, ADGM's best-in-class regulatory system and SSE's position as one of the largest and fastest growing global exchange. This international exchange will fulfill the investment and financing needs for issuers, investors and market participants within the MENA region, along the Belt-

and-Road route, and globally. Third, in May 2018, SSE and SZSE inked an agreement to acquire 25% equity of Dhaka Stock Exchange. In May 2017, SSE and Moscow Exchange (MOEX) inked a strategic cooperation agreement; in June 2017, SSE and Astana International Financial Centre Authority of Kazakhstan signed an agreement to co-invest in building the Astana International Exchange. As an international financial center, Shanghai is on its way to build a network of stock exchanges along the Belt and Road.

5) Promoting cooperation on and development of commodity market under the Belt and Road Initiative

Shanghai is making efforts to build a host of authoritative commodity e-commerce platforms, negotiate with countries and regions along the Belt and Road on establishing the pricing and trading mechanism for major commodities such as energy, steel, gold, precious metal, cotton and soybean, forming a "Shanghai Index" with international influence and promoting the RMB pricing and settlement of commodities. On 26 March 2018, the Shanghai International Energy Exchange launched trading of RMB-denominated crude oil futures contracts, which is conducive to improving the existing international crude oil pricing system and international currency system and allowing overseas investors and institutions from countries, those along the Belt and Road in particular, to participate in the Chinese market. On 9 April 2017, DGCX listed the Shanghai Gold Futures Contract, marking the first-ever application of the Shanghai Gold Benchmark Price in international financial markets. In 2017, Shanghai OTC Commodity Derivatives Association (SOCDA) and Saint Petersburg International Mercantile Exchange (SPIMEX) inked a memorandum of understanding to build a platform for exchange between Chinese and Russian commodity enterprises.

4.4.3 Establishing functional systems of an international financial center to serve the Belt and Road Initiative

With the four functions of Shanghai International Financial Center in terms of serving the Belt and Road Initiative, it is necessary for Shanghai to leverage its special status as an international financial center to build a series of service platforms and mechanism and form a service functional system (see fig. 4 - 1).

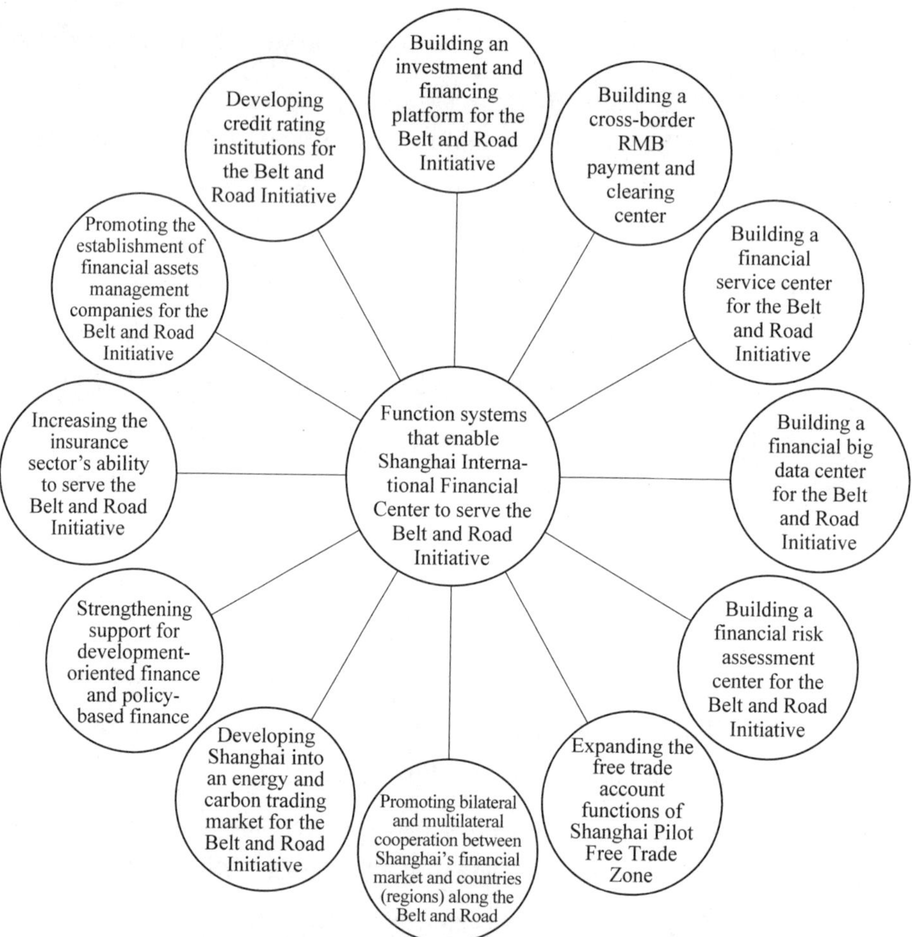

Fig. 4 - 1 Functions systems that enable Shanghai International Financial Center to serve the Belt and Road Initiative

1) Building an investment and financing platform for the Belt and Road Initiative

First, Shanghai will establish an investment and financing platform under the Belt and Road Initiative for Chinese enterprises and investors, and use it to facilitate investment in countries and regions along the Belt and Road. Such platform is open to domestic enterprises and investors, and the money raised on it will be used for infrastructure projects under the Belt and Road Initiative. Under the investment and financing platform for the Belt and Road Initiative, Chinese enterprises can raise money by setting up special funds, borrowing from banks, issuing or increasing the issue of shares, or issuing bonds. It is necessary align the financing system for domestic enterprises with the Belt and Road Initiative, and it is necessary to make an institutional arrangement that enterprise borrowing, enterprise IPO, additional issue and issue of corporate bonds should meet the needs of the Initiative. Second, a financing platform for enterprises and governments from countries along the Belt and Road will be established in Shanghai International Financial Center, allowing overseas enterprises and governments to finance under the Initiative. It is open to overseas non-resident enterprises, and the financing projects will be used for infrastructure construction under the Initiative. For example, Shanghai will support countries (regions) along the Belt and Road in issuing Panda Bonds and other RMB securities products in Shanghai, and support overseas quality enterprises' efforts to seek development through Shanghai's capital market.

2) Building a cross-border RMB payment and clearing center

Building a cross-border RMB payment and clearing center is aimed to promote the use of RMB in trade, industrial investment and financial investment in countries (regions) along the route. China has set up the CIPS, and it is viable to further the Phase II of CIPS to establish a linked currency clearing mechanism with clearing institutions from countries (regions) along the route. In the CIPS system, Shanghai International Financial Center can build a module that is dedicated to serving the cross-border RMB clearing under the Initiative. As an international financial center, Shanghai will encourage financial institutions from countries (regions) along the Belt and Road to set up clearing branches, step up cooperation between Chinese and foreign commercial banks, and include them into our clearing system. Shanghai will support UnionPay International and other non-bank payment institutions in providing cross-border financial services to introduce inclusive finance, represented by Internet and mobile payment, to countries (regions) along the route. Meanwhile, Shanghai will explore the establishment of CCDC Shanghai headquarters, set up a cross-border issue platform for RMB bonds, and promote cooperation and exchange between Shanghai Clearing House and foreign clearing institutions.

3) Building a professional financial service center for the Belt and Road Initiative

The professional financial service center provides a series of professional supporting services to serve and promote investment and financing activities under the Initiative, so it is closely linked with the investment and financing center for the Initiative. As the sole international financial center in Mainland China, Shanghai's advanced professional financial services constitute the preconditions for becoming a financial service center for the Initiative for Shanghai. The financial service center mainly provides such financial services as insurance, financing guarantee, financial lease, credit rating, financial consulting and financial talent training. For example, insuring investment projects under the Belt and Road Initiative is conducive to their smooth progress. Financial lease service, project financing lease in particular, is one of the important means to conduct infrastructure investment under the Initiative. Shanghai enjoys exceptional advantages in financial consulting and financial talent training. Therefore, developing related financial talents should become an important task for Shanghai in terms of participating in the Belt and Road Initiative.

4) Establishing a financial big data center for the Belt and Road Initiative

The establishment of a financial big data center for the Initiative can offer conditions for the optimum match between capital demand and supply. China has seen various Belt and Road databases across the country. For example, Shanghai Academy of Social Sciences established a Belt and Road big database; Alibaba has decided to invest in the establishment of a Belt and Road data center in Dubai; Social Sciences Academic Press launched a Belt and Road special database; Xinhua News Agency launched the Xinhua Silk Road commercial database; the International Academy of the Belt and Road, a private think tank, set up a Belt and Road eco-social development database; and the State Information Center launched a Belt and Road big data center. However, there is no special database for the financial field. It is viable for Shanghai to build a financial big data center open to the country and beyond, which mainly serves the financial investment and financing business under the Initiative and provides information for participating financiers and investors.

5) Building a financial risk assessment center for the Belt and Road Initiative

Given the scale of infrastructure construction involved in the implementation of the Initiative, financing is required via the financial market. Whether enterprises and investors are willing to participate in these investment projects depends on the assessment of investment risks to a certain extent. If enterprises and investors can identify profitable and secure projects through financial risk assessment, the Initiative will attract a large amount of subsequent funds; if enterprises and investors suffer losses due to unexpected risks, it is difficult to sustain the Initiative. As such, the establishment of a Belt and Road financial risk assessment center in Shanghai is highly relevant. As an international financial center,

Shanghai could develop a large number of professional institutions and talents to conduct financial risk assessment on projects under the Initiative. In the meantime, Shanghai should step up its cooperation with domestic and foreign financial institutions. Policy banks such as CDB and the Export-Import Bank of China (CEXIM), which have long invested in the countries along the Belt and Road, have effective risk assessment systems in place. The World Bank (WB), the Asian Development Bank (ADB) and other international financial institutions, which have long invested in infrastructure projects in the countries and regions along the Belt and Road, have accumulated abundant experience in risk assessment. For Shanghai to establish a Belt and Road financial risk assessment center, it is important to give full play to the above-mentioned resources.

6) Expanding the free trade account functions of Shanghai Pilot Free Trade Zone

On 22 April 2015, the Shanghai Head Office of the People's Bank of China issued the Notice on Activating Foreign Currency Services under Free Trade Accounts, making an official announcement that financial institutions engaging in separate accounting services in Shanghai pilot free trade zone can provide domestic and foreign currency integrated financial services under free trade accounts for entities within its jurisdiction and abroad. This marks the formal activation of foreign currency services under free trade accounts. Free trade accounts can support other pilot free trade zones in China and countries (regions) along the route in capitalizing on the free trade accounts of Shanghai pilot free trade zone, provide participating enterprises and their employees with relevant cross-border financial services, and offer services regarding the convenient settlement and convertibility of cross-border funds for various entities with free trade accounts. Therefore, expanding the free trade account function of Shanghai pilot free trade zone can help Shanghai better serve the Belt and

Road Initiative.

7) Promoting bilateral and multilateral cooperation between Shanghai's financial market and countries (regions) along the Belt and Road

Shanghai may consider stepping up its cooperation with the central cities in nearly 60 countries and regions along the Belt and Road, including transportation hubs, international economic and financial centers. Shanghai could explore financial cooperation agreements with major financial centers in the countries along the Belt and Road for cooperation on project financing, settlement and clearing, credit guarantee and risk sharing. These efforts include supporting the bilateral business and equity cooperation between Shanghai's financial market and the exchanges and registration and clearing institutions in countries (regions) along the route; advancing the international board of Shanghai Gold Exchange and Shanghai Gold pricing mechanism, promoting business connection and industrial cooperation with countries (regions) in the countries along the route, and enhancing RMB's influence as a gold pricing mechanism; building a reinsurance platform of Shanghai Insurance Exchange, exploring the establishment of a reinsurance consortium for the Belt and Road Initiative, and encouraging SHFE to open transaction warehouses overseas. A mechanism should be established for cooperation between Shanghai's financial market and the financial centers in countries (regions) along the Belt and Road, as this can substantiate the financial cooperation between financial centers, and further enhance Shanghai's influence, leadership and status as an international financial center, while serving the Belt and Road Initiative.

8) Developing Shanghai into an energy and carbon trading market for the Belt and Road Initiative

As an important junction of the Belt and Road and the Yangtze River Economic Zone as well as the terminal with the largest container handling capacity, Shanghai enjoys exceptional geographical advantages. Therefore, Shanghai's carbon market should actively engage in exchange and communication on climate change with neighboring provinces and cities, leverage its role as a pilot project on the basis of its own market building experience, and strive to foster sound competition and cooperation with neighboring countries and regions via the Yangtze River Economic Zone, thus giving full play to its radiation function and driving the comprehensive upgrade of industrial chain in Yangtze River region and the leapfrog development of financial sector. To build a Belt and Road energy and carbon trade market, Shanghai needs to rely on such platforms as INE and Shanghai Petroleum and Natural Gas Exchange (SHPGX), launch crude oil futures, create synergy with countries (regions) along the route in the markets of energy spot, futures trade, carbon trade and technology exchange, and enhance its international influence.

9) Strengthening support for development-oriented finance and policy-based finance

Increasing the support for open finance and policy-based finance calls for CDB to increase special loan support for Shanghai-backed projects concerning infrastructure, financial cooperation and production capacity cooperation in the countries (regions) along the route, so as to expand the issurance of special bonds for the Belt and Road Initiative. It also calls for CEXIM to increase loan support for Shanghai-backed projects in the countries (regions) along the route to increase the issurance of preferential loans. Shanghai should develop financial products for long-term investment and large-scale investment. The Belt and Road Initiative is meant to encourage infrastructure investment, which features long investment period and large investment demand. As such, relevant financial innovation concerning the Belt and Road Initiative should focus on two "translations", that is, how to translate short-term funds into long-term investment funds and how to translate private scattered funds into investment funds for large projects. To this end, capital market with relevantly sophisticated secondary market should be fully utilized. In addition, converting private scattered capital to investment funds for large projects requires PPP model to give full play to the role of private capital. Shanghai should reach out to unilateral and multilateral financial institutions participating in the Belt and Road Initiative, encourage international development-oriented financial institutions concerning the Initiative and commercial financial institutions in countries (regions) along the route to open branches, and support the establishment of private equity funds and venture capital funds under the Initiative.

10) Increasing the insurance sector's ability to serve the Belt and Road Initiative

In the process of going global under the Belt and Road Initiative, Chinese enterprises are facing increasing uncertainties, due to restrictions of different political systems, economic and legal environments in the countries and regions along the Belt and Road. To solve this problem, diversified and personalized financial services are required to assist enterprises in optimizing their investment and financing structure and strengthening active risk management. As an important component of financial services, export credit insurance can effectively serve the major components of the Initiative, including facility and trade connectivity, provide risk guarantee and financing support for China's "go global" strategy, and reflect the unique role of policy-oriented financial service institutions in foreign trade. As a kind of policy-oriented insurance, export credit insurance can effectively prevent international trade risks, and protect against buyer credit risks and national sovereign risks. This calls for China Export & Credit Insurance Corporation to extend the coverage of credit insurance to the financing of key areas through Shanghai-back projects abroad. Shanghai needs to make great efforts to develop overseas insurance, cargo transportation insurance and engineering construction insurance, so as to provide omnidirectional insurance guarantee for the Belt and Road Initiative.

11) Promoting the establishment of financial assets management companies for the Belt and Road Initiative

Financial assets management companies have three roles to play in advancing the Belt and Road Initiative: first, with non-performing asset business as the core, they can identify new ways to address non-performing assets, so as to optimize the allocation of economic resources; second, with a focus on serving the real economy, they can commit themselves to the structural reform of supply side to increase the flow orderliness of economic factors; third, they can strengthen international economic policy study, deepen international cooperation, and build a multi-level financial business platform. Therefore, establishing the Belt and Road financial assets management companies in Shanghai calls for the city to support qualified financial institutions in opening financial assets management companies in Shanghai pilot free trade zone, so as to optimize the financial assets allocation for the Belt and Road Initiative. It also calls for Shanghai to explore the pilot program of overseas credit assets securitization, and encourage the participation of overseas financial institutions and institutional investors.

12) Developing credit rating institutions for the Belt and Road Initiative

In terms of the construction, investment and financing under the Belt and Road Initiative, it is imperative to identify country-based sovereign credit risks. The countries and regions along the Belt and Road, including China, increasingly demand and rely on independent, object, unbiased and effective sovereign credit rating. Accordingly, sovereign rating risks will increase. In such context, we should take preventive measures as early as possible, to ensure the financial security of our country and promote construction and cooperation on the Initiative. To develop Belt and Road credit rating institutions, Shanghai needs to encourage qualified enterprises to conduct credit rating on the countries (regions) along the route, and gradually develop credit rating institutions and systems with international influence.

4.5 Advancing RMB Internationalization

2018 marks the 40th anniversary of reform and opening-up. Looking in the future, with China's growing global status and economic significance, increasing the openness of the financial sector not only constitutes an important component of China's opening-up efforts in the new era, but also represents the inherent requirement for the development of the financial sector itself. Therefore, it gains more profound significance. Underpinned by the Belt and Road Initiative, financial opening-up is of great importance in terms of advancing RMB internationalization, encouraging full competition on the financial market, increasing the efficiency of financial market, and boosting China's competitiveness as a global player.

4.5.1 New progress in RMB internationalization

According to the 2018 Q1 China Monetary Policy Execution Report issued by the People's Bank of China, China has seen further improvement of the policy on cross-border use of RMB, continued improvement of relevant infrastructure and new progress in RMB internationalization. According to the central bank's financial statistics report, in 2017, RMB settlement of cross-border trade reached CNY 4.36 trillion, and RMB settlement of direct investment was CNY 1.64 trillion. In particular, RMB settlement of cross-border trade in goods and services, other current account items, ODI, and FDI amounted to CNY 3.27 trillion, CNY 1.09 trillion, CNY 456.88 billion and CNY 1.18 trillion.

(1) Bond Connect activated Chinese market to open new channels to satisfy demands for RMB assets investment. In 2017, overseas institutions added CNY 37.7 billion of RMB bonds, making the total exceed CNY 1 trillion for the first time to CNY 1.15 trillion at the end of the year, and setting a new record in history. The proportion of overseas institutions in China's domestic bond market increased to 1.99% from 1.26% at the end of 2016. Since 2017, Bloomberg Barclays and Citibank incorporated Chinese bonds into global bond index, marking the increasing demands of the international market for RMB assets.

(2) The median price quotation mechanism introduced the "inverse periodic factor", and the RMB exchange rate gain strength while maintaining stability. In 2017, the reform of RMB exchange rate formation mechanism was deepened, and the exchange rate formation mechanism of "closing rate + a basket of currency exchange rate changes + inverse periodic factor" operated in an orderly manner. Supported by such factors as steady growth of China's economy, weakening USD, wider interest margin between China and US and the incorporation of the "inverse periodic factor" into the medium price mechanism, the CNY-USD exchange rate witnesses the largest increase in the recent nine years, ending the trend of continuous decline over the past three years. On the basis of being generally strong, RMB exchange rate may experience significant increase of two-way fluctuation, which creates a favorable environment for RMB internationalization.

(3) 2017 saw a turning point for cross-border capital flows, and the foreign exchange management policy was neutralized. With macro-prudential management playing an increasingly strong role in cross-border

capital flow, 2017 witnessed the transition of China's cross-border capital flowing from net outflow to basic balance. The foreign currency reserve was increased by USD 129.432 billion, realizing the first annual growth over the recent three years.

(4) Off-shore RMB service rebounded, and diversified tools were launched for RMB risk management. In 2017, with the improvement of RMB fundamentals, overseas institutions gained confidence about holding RMB gradually, resulting in a steady rise in the scale of off-shore RMB deposit. By the end of December 2017, RMB deposit in Hong Kong SAR reached CNY 559.1 billion, an increase of 2.3% over the end of previous year and an increase of 10.2% over the start of the year. In 2017, RMB deposit in Taiwan Region increased by CNY 10.837 billion, an increase of 3.48% year on year. By the end of September 2017, RMB deposit in Singapore was CNY 139 billion, an increase of 10.32% over the end of previous year. RMB has become one of the most actively traded currencies on the global foreign exchange market, and London is the largest off-shore RMB exchange trading center. In the meantime, Hong Kong Exchanges and Clearing Limited (HKEX) launched such products as RMB option, RMB gold futures, the pilot project of five-year government bond futures contract of the Ministry of Finance, advancing the transition towards risk management, cross-border capital allocation, RMB assets management and product innovation. In 2017, the limit for RMB Qualified Foreign Institutional Investors (RQFII) in Hong Kong was increased to CNY 500 billion. The People's Bank of China and the Hong Kong Monetary Authority (HKMA) signed a renewed currency swap agreement of RMB 400 billion/HK$ 470 billion.

(5) IMF released the world's holdings of RMB denominated foreign exchange reserves for the first time, and RMB was identified in reserve currencies. Since its inclusion in the basket of currencies that make up the

Special Drawing Right (SDR), RMB has gained greater influence and recognition worldwide, and its share in the allocation of foreign exchange reserves of central banks across the globe has increased at a fast speed. In March 2017, IMF announced RMB denominated foreign exchange reserves for the first time. By Q3 2017, RMB foreign exchange reserves reached USD 1.08 trillion, an increase of USD 17.16 billion over the end of 2016, accounting for 1. 12% of allocated foreign exchange reserves. In the meantime, following the European Central Bank's announcement on an investment equivalent to 500 million euros of its foreign reserves in RMB, Deutsche Bundesbank and Banque de France decided to identify RMB in their foreign exchange reserves. At present, over 60 countries and regions have included RMB into their foreign exchange reserves, underpinning RMB's increasing importance in the global financial system. RMB's role as an international reserve currency has achieved initial progress.

(6) China promoted green finance across the globe, and provided quality RMB assets to the world. Since 2016, China has carried out international multilateral and bilateral cooperation at different levels and on multiple platforms, with increasing influence in the field of green finance around the globe. Chinese-funded enterprises issuers have also gained influence on the international green bond market furtherly. Since the inception of China's green bond market in 2016, by the end of 2017, a total of 184 bonds have been issued in China and beyond, with a total amount of CNY 479.9 billion, accounting for about 27% of the total across the world. In China, 167 bonds have been issued, with the total amount exceeding CNY 400 billion and reaching CNY 409. 7 billion. Both the green finance and RMB internalization are important state strategies, which embody the combination of reform, innovation and opening-up. With the constant advance of opening-up, RMB denominated green assets have become a more valuable target of investment for the world. At

present, by demonstrating its influence in the field of green finance around the world, China is gradually gaining voice in global economic and financial governance, which is equally important to advancing RMB internationalization. China's efforts to develop green finance conform to the trend of time, and are conducive to increasing the acceptance of RMB on the international market.

(7) With a focus on the construction of CIPS and interconnection platform, RMB payment network was extended around the world. The previous year witnessed progress in the development CIPS, interconnection platform and other key projects. Domestic third-party payment leaders, represented by Alipay and Wechat Pay, are expanding their business and user base around the globe. On May 2, 2018, the Phase 2 of CIPS was fully launched, with eligible direct participants engaged online simultaneously. CIPS, as an important financial infrastructure developed in line with international standards, provides fund clearing and settlement services to domestic and foreign participants in cross-border RMB businesses, serving as a "highway" for RMB internationalization. As of the end of March 2018, a total of 31 domestic and foreign direct participants, as well as 695 domestic and foreign indirect participants have joined CIPS expanding its actual business scope to 148 countries and jurisdictions. Meanwhile, Fin Tech is advancing the "last mile" connectivity of RMB business. Alipay has around 450 million users worldwide, and Wechat has 980 million users across the globe. Over 120,000 physical stores in 26 markets in Europe, North America, East Asia and Southeast Asia accept payment via Alipay, and Wechat Pay provides payment services in 12 currencies for 15 countries and regions. With the support of third-party payment platforms, RMB payment is increasingly expanded to e-commerce, education and other service-oriented export sectors outside China. With the rapid development of third-party payment in China, the interconnection platform has

emerged. Underpinned by mobile payment represented by Alipay and Wechat Pay as well as the settlement system guaranteed by the interconnection platform, the RMB payment and clearing system will be improved and become more convenient.

(8) The infrastructure for "Oil RMB" was further improved, gaining say in commodity pricing. With the economic and financial security and stability of oil traders being challenged under the single dollar system and economic stability being impacted by dollar fluctuations, it is an irresistible trend to create a diversified oil pricing and settlement system. In August 2017, following a new round of restrictions imposed by US, Venezuela made an announcement on replacing USD with a basket of currencies, including RMB, and began pricing bilateral oil trade in RMB. In October 2017, the China Foreign Exchange Trade System (CFETS) launched a payment-versus-payment system for RMB and ruble transactions, marking an improvement of the bilateral infrastructure of "Oil RMB" between China and Russia. In March 2018, crude oil futures were launched on Shanghai Futures Exchange. "Oil RMB" will not only serve as a starting point for comprehensive opening-up of China's futures market, but also carry the important tasks of striving for commodity pricing right and promoting RMB internationalization.

(9) Increasing inter-bank foreign exchange market regional exchange currency pairs helped with the use of RMB across the globe. To improve the financial sector's ability to serve the Belt and Road Initiative, help market entities avoid exchange rate risks and promote the use of RMB in bilateral trade and investment, CFETS launched inter-bank foreign exchange market regional transactions in RMB and Mongolian Tugrik in August and those in RMB and Cambodian Riel in September, increasing the number of RMB regional exchange currency pairs to 4, in light of the current inter-bank regional transactions in RMB and Thai Baht as well as

in RMB and Kazakhstani Tenge. The launching of regional currency pair transactions in Yunnan, Xinjiang, Inner Mongolia and Guangxi represents the improvement of the Belt and Road mechanism, which can break the middle link in foreign currency convertibility and help save the cost of exchange. This not only is of great importance in terms of advancing the facilitation of local currency settlement of trade and investment between China and other countries and improving the financial sector's ability to serve the real economy, but also blazes a new trail for the border financial sector to serve ASEAN and support regional economic development. Regional currency pair transactions are beneficial to RMB output, further promoting RMB internationalization.

4.5.2 New business pivots to promote RMB internationalization through opening-up and innovation

The recent three years have witnessed a decline in cross-border RMB payment, share of global payment and settlement and overseas deposit. Cross-border trade settlement in RMB dropped from CNY 7.23 trillion to CNY 5.23 trillion, and then to CNY 4.36 trillion; direct investment settlement in RMB rose from CNY 2.32 trillion to CNY 2.46 trillion before dropping to CNY 1.64 trillion. In terms of the ranking of RMB payment, according to the Society for Worldwide Interbank Financial Telecommunication (SWIFT), RMB was the world's fifth largest payment current by the end of December 2015; at the end of December 2016, RMB was the world's sixth largest payment currency, with its market sharing dropping to 1.68%; at the end of Q3 2017, RMB accounted for 1.70% of global payment settlement. In terms of deposit, RMB deposit in Hong Kong SAR, a major overseas RMB off-shore market, reached 1 trillion in 2014 at its peak; at the end of 2016, it was 546.7 billion; at the end of Q2 2017, RMB deposit of institutions in Hong Kong SAR was CNY 535.5

billion, nearly decreasing to half of its peak.

Despite being the result of the combination of various factors, these ups and downs demonstrate the long-term and arduous nature of the RMB internationalization process. At present, it is imperative to find ways to deepen reform and opening-up, so as to make new breakthroughs and add new driving force to the cross-border RMB business. In 2018, as the reform and opening-up of China's economy is deepened, the cross-border RMB business should follow policy reform breakthrough as its driving force, align with the two pivots of the Belt and Road Initiative and commodity trade, and proceed steadily through adjustment.

1) Pivot I: Belt and Road investment

Since the Belt and Road Initiative was proposed, China has inked cooperative agreements with over 80 countries and organizations, and carried out institutionalized production capacity cooperation with over 30 countries and regions. In the first 11 months of 2017, Chinese enterprises increased their investment in 59 countries and regions along the Belt and Road, and direct investment reached USD 12.4 billion; the countries and regions along the route invested USD 5 billion in China, and opened over 3,500 enterprises. In the first 11 months of 2017, Chinese enterprises inked USD 113.53 worth of new foreign engineering contracts with 61 countries and regions related to the Belt and Road. Moreover, Chinese enterprises are advancing the establishment of 75 overseas business and trade cooperative zones in the countries and regions along the Belt and Road, attracting nearly 3,500 enterprises.

With the advance of the Belt and Road Initiative, overseas financial infrastructure that is conducive to the development of overseas RMB has score remarkable progress. For example, 42 members of Chinese-funded banks are the countries and regions along the Belt and Road; the capital scale of the Silk Road Fund reached USD 40 billion; 6 Chinese banks have established more than 80 subsidiaries, branches and representative offices in 19 countries and regions along the route; China UnionPay has covered over 50 countries and regions along the route; China Export & Credit Insurance Corporation provides various insurance services for cooperative projects in about 20 countries along the route.

Currently, initial progress has been made in the industrial development and financial infrastructure construction in the countries and regions along the Belt and Road. This represents the most direct, important and solid foundation for RMB internalization. The relevant business is where cross-border RMB can be utilized most effectively. This will drive the rapid growth of cross-border RMB.

2) Pivot II: Commodity trade

The field of commodity trade is another business pivot for cross-border RMB. In 2017, the total volume of China's commodity import and export was CNY 27.79 trillion, increasing by 14.2% compared to that of 2016, reversing the trend of continuous decline over the past two years The quantity and price of commodity import was improved, and the import quantum of various commodities created a new record in the history. In 2017, China's import of iron ores and crude oil created a new record. With the increasingly demands for coal and LNG, the import quantum of such commodities accounted for a large proportion in the world.

In China, as the largest trade importer, RMB accounts for a low proportion of settlement for purchasing commodities, because the country lacks the rights of pricing and settlement currency option. The choice of settlement currency depends to a certain degree on the supply and demand. In a cycle of weak commodity trade, supply exceeds demand on the international market, giving us more say as a buyer. At this stage, if we can seize the opportunity to increase the proportion of RMB settlement in the field of commodities, this will not only help Chinese importers avoid risks associated with exchange rate, but also be conducive to giving play to the international commodity pricing function of internationalized RMB, thus enhancing the international acceptance of RMB.

China has begun to adopt RMB pricing in some areas of commodity. For example, China launched RMB denominated crude oil futures contract, by means of which domestic buyers of crude oil futures will lock the price of crude oil and conduct crude oil futures transactions in local currency through INE. Shanghai Clearing House launched RMB ethylene glycol swap central counterpart clearing business, which not only meets relevant enterprises' demands for hedging, but also is conducive to filling the gap in Shanghai's financial factor market, thus playing a role in developing Shanghai into a global center of RMB innovation, trade, pricing and clearing.

China's demands for commodity import have significantly influenced the international commodity market, providing foundation and conditions for RMB pricing in the field of commodity. To avoid exchange rate risks, Chinese enterprises engaging in trade also have actual demands for RMB pricing. Despite USD being the major pricing currency in commodity transactions, nothing is in the way of RMB being increasingly used as a pricing currency for goods. The commodity trade will serve as an effective pivot for cross-border RMB to advance cross-border RMB payment and RMB internalization.

References

[1] 2017 Development Report of International Financial Center [M]. Beijing: China Financial Publishing House, 2017.

[2] China (Shenzhen) Development Institute. China's Financial Center Index (CDI CFCI 9) Zooms in Xi'an [M]. Beijing: Economic Press China, 2017.

[3] Chu Minwei, Wu Daqi, He Ying. 2013 Blue Book on Development of Shanghai as International Financial Center [M]. Shanghai: Shanghai People's Publishing House, 2013.

[4] Chu Minwei, Wu Daqi, He Ying. 2012 Blue Book on Development of Shanghai as International Financial Center [M]. Shanghai: Shanghai People's Publishing House, 2012.

[5] Li Qiang. Speech at The Mobilization Meeting for The Implementation of "Shanghai City Master Plan (2017 - 2035)"[N]. Liberation Daily.

[6] Liu Yong. Us priority: influence of trump's tax reform policy on world economy [J]. Red Flag Manuscript, 2018(1): 30 - 32.

[7] Li Xunlei, et al. The Development Strategy of Shanghai as an International Financial Center in 2020 [M]. Beijing: China Financial Publishing House, 2016.

[8] Wang Zhen. Annual Report on Development of Yangtze River Economic Belt (2011 - 2015) [M]. Beijing: Social Sciences Academic Press (China), 2016.

[9] Wu Daqi. 2014 Blue Book on Development of Shanghai as International Financial Center [M]. Shanghai : Shanghai People's Publishing House, 2014.

[10] Wu Daqi. 2015 Blue Book on Development of Shanghai as International Financial Center [M]. Shanghai : Shanghai People's Publishing House, 2015.

[11] Wu Daqi. 2016 Blue Book on Development of Shanghai as International Financial Center [M]. Shanghai: Shanghai People's Publishing House, 2016.

[12] Wu Daqi. 2017 Blue Book on Development of Shanghai as International Financial Center [M]. Shanghai: Shanghai People's Publishing House, 2018.

[13] Xi Jinping. Keynote Address at the Opening Ceremony of The 2018 Annual Meeting of The Bo'ao Forum for Asia [N]. People's Daily, 2018 - 04 - 11.

[14] Xi Jinping. Speech at the Symposium on Promoting the Development of the Yangtze River Economic Belt [OL]. Xinhua Net.

[15] Xi Jinping. Speech on Celebrating The 30th Anniversary of Hainan's Establishment of A Special Economic Zone [N]. People's Daily, 2018 - 04 - 13.